God's World

STUDIES IN MIDDLE EASTERN LITERATURES — NUMBER TWO

God's World

by

Nagib Mahfuz

An Anthology of Short Stories
Translated from the Arabic by

AKEF ABADIR and ROGER ALLEN

BIBLIOTHECA ISLAMICA
Minneapolis

ISBN: 0-88297-044-5 (paperbound)
ISBN: 0-88297-047-X (clothbound)

BIBLIOTHECA ISLAMICA, INC.
Box 14474
Minneapolis, MN 55414
U.S.A.

Contents

Introduction

Nagib Mahfuz has written novels, short stories and plays. In certain novels (and particularly those from the earlier period – 1939-1957) the characters are depicted in some detail. In the short stories, on the other hand, they emerge in a more abstract form, something which would seem to reflect much of twentieth century fiction, in that man is often portrayed in terse but penetrating detail. Like Camus, Sartre and even Edward Albee, Mahfuz is writing what is frequently termed *litterature des Idées*.

Many people acknowledge Mahfuz to be one of the masters of the novel and short story in the Arab world today, and he has often been said to belong to this same school of writers. However, there are at least two ways in which he differs from his European contemporaries. Firstly his point of departure is different; this not only in the more obvious aspects such as language, religion and tradition, but also, more importantly, in intellectual heritage. Before the modern renaissance in the Arab intellectual world, the literary tradition had produced no works of any originality for several centuries, and the new genres which had been imported from the West were still in the process of assimilation at the beginning of this century. In writing works of prose fiction, Mahfuz has made use of techniques and patterns from a variety of literary schools and movements; his novels show quite clearly the various stages of this development. This in fact marks one of the main differences between his works and those of European writers such as Camus. For, while in Europe the novelistic tradition has evolved over an extended period through a number of different movements –

romantic, realistic, symbolistic – in the Arab world it is virtually only since the beginning of this century that novelists have begun to write works in this genre on the twofold base of a revived classical prose tradition and translations and imitations of European models. Of necessity therefore, this has been an accelerated, compressed process, one in which few writers have shown a mastery of all aspects of the art of prose fiction. When one of the characters in Mahfuz's latest work, *Mirrors* (1972), records that "the Arab world has to cover a period of five or six centuries in a quarter of a century", he is referring to a wider process than that of literature alone, and yet the implications are the same, although the time periods may be different.

To many Western writers of recent times – particuarly those mentioned above – literature has a function and a message to convey; their task seems somewhat analogous with that of the ancient philosophers, namely to present some kind of explanation for life, for the secret motivations which make man function in this universe. For Camus, for example, this study focuses on revolt. Beginning with Epicurus and materializing in the eighteenth century, it finally finds in Camus the the student of revolt. Camus's major aim is to explain the motives behind our lives, his own motives for writing, and the meaning behind some of his more famous stories. *The Rebel*, for example, is not simply a collection of articles, but an explanation of what he has read and written; the motives of Sisyphus in his futile attempts to climb the mountain cannot be fully com-prehended unless one reads *The Rebel*. Sartre too has his own ideas which he proceeds to explain through the medium of novels and plays. Many other writers have followed the same process.

Mahfuz has done none of these things. The Arab world has not been without writers who were prepared to write works like *The Rebel* in which they elaborate on their own ideas and philosophies. For example, Taufiq al-Hakim, the great dramatist, wrote a book in which he tried to explain the import of many of his works under the title *Equiibri-*

the Egyptian population, the *fellahin* or peasants, are not represented nor is the "oppressed" person in general. To be sure, there are characters who are poor; 'Uncle' Ibrahim in *God's World*, for instance, works all his life as an office boy for a paltry salary. He is a poor man, and yet he is much better off than a large percentage of the population. These people struggle from one day to the next to survive. Early in their lives, they learn some habits which enable them to continue life's struggle, but their intellect remains unchallenged and they are simply left with instincts to motivate their lives. In the final group, a few stories dealing with such people are included. In *The Prisoner of War's Uniform*, Gahsha (a word which means "little donkey") is a man of meagre intelligence, born with little chance in life. His aspirations are as low as his social status. All his energy goes into the struggle to survive without realizing the absurdity of it all or looking for any kind of consolation. His one hope and ambition is to survive. The tragedy of the second world war passes right in front of his eyes, and yet he does not care who is fighting whom, who won, who lost, or why his own country is being occupied. An insignificant person, he is motivated only by his own instincts. The main character in *The Wilderness* perhaps shows the depths of such petty concerns. He can spend almost his entire life on a stupid quest motivated by hate, jealousy and revenge without ever being able to look beyond the confining limits of his own hatred. After being forced to divorce his young wife on their wedding night, he loses every faculty except that of planning his revenge. It is the characters in situations and environments such as these who are perhaps most representative of the Egyptian flavour among the stories in this collection.

God's World

Activity began in the secretarial department when 'Uncle' Ibrahim, the office boy, came in. He opened the windows one after another and started sweeping the big floor with an air of almost total disinterest. He shook his head with a slow regularity, and his lips kept moving as though he were chewing something. This movement made the white hairs on his chin and cheeks stand up; his head, on the other hand, didn't have a single hair on top. He brushed the dust off the desk tops and arranged the dossiers and instruments. After all that, he took a comprehensive look at the entire room – the department – and moved from one desk to another as though he could see the people who worked at them. At one moment, he seemed to be satisfied and then he looked exasperated; he smiled once and then went away. Now it's time to go and get their breakfast, he told himself.

Mr. Ahmad, the archive clerk, was the first to arrive. He was getting old, about fifty, and his face wore a permanent look of annoyance as though it were a scroll recorded on the bark of time itself. He was followed by Mr. Mustafa, the clerk at the typewriter who laughed a lot; but it was just a nervous laugh which simply covered up his everyday worries. Then came Samir, or the mystery man as he was known in the department; the soldier whose smiling features showed clearly that he had yet to emerge from the joys of childhood. Mr. Lutfi came swaggering in, well-dressed and wearing a ring, watch and tiepin all made of gold. Close behind him came Hammam, slightly built and self-centered. Finally in came the departmental director, Professor Kamil, enveloped in a personal halo of dignity and carrying a rosary.

The office buzzed with the sound of voices and rustling papers, but no one started working. Even the director started talking on the telephone. Immediately newspapers were hoisted into the air like so many flags. Lutfi was following the news:

"The end of the world will be this year," he said. The director raised his voice over the telephone. "How can you deny the obvious?" he asked in delight.

"Why do we all put up with the miseries of marriage and children?" Samir asked. "Here's a young man killing his father with his mother watching!"

"What's the point of writing a prescription?" asked Ahmad with a croaking voice, "if the medicine isn't on the market?"

From where he was sitting, the soldier kept looking through the window at a doctor's clinic in the opposite building; he was waiting for the blonde German nurse to appear at the window.

"Believe me," Lutfi continued confidently, "the end of the world's nearer than you think...."

The director put his hand over the mouthpiece and gave Hammam an order. "Prepare file 1-3/130 this year...." he said. He then resumed his love chat on the phone. Hammam didn't look up from his paper but merely muttered between his teeth: "Son of a bitch!"

Ibrahim came back with a full tray and started handing out *ful,** ta'miyya'*** cheese sandwiches and crushed *tahini* sweets. They began to munch the food and the sound of lips smacking reverberated round the room; their eyes meanwhile remained glued to the news. Ibrahim stood at the entrance to the department watching them eating with a strange bewildered look in his eye.

"'Uncle' Ibrahim, get our salaries," Ahmad yelled at him

* Beans
** Fried beans

with his mouth full of food.

He went away. An hour later, a tie and perfume sales-man who visited the department regularly at the beginning of each month came in and went around the desks showing his wares. The civil servants started looking at them and some of them took what they needed. The salesman went away on the understanding that he would come back when they got their salaries. After another hour, the butter seller came to collect the amounts he was owed, but Mustafa laughingly explained to him that he should wait till 'Uncle' Ibrahim came back.

The man waited at the door, his lips moving in a non-stop recitation. The typewriter was clacking away busily, and Samir went into the director's office to show him some im-portant papers. For the first time, the sun came in through the window which looked out on the square. The soldier kept on stealing glances in the direction of the clinic win-dow. The director yelled for 'Uncle' to do something for him, but Mustafa reminded him that he had not returned from the cashier's office yet. At this point, Ahmad looked up from the files. "The man's late!", he said. "Why is he so late?"

The butter seller went to the other offices, then he would be back. Ahmad went outside the room, looked left and right along the passageway and then came back. "There's no sign of him," he said. "What's holding him up, the old windbag!?"

When the third hour went by, Ahmad lost patience. He got up and announced in a loud voice that he was going to the cashier's office to look for him. He came back looking very angry. "He took the money a full hour ago," he said. "Where's the fool gone?"

"Did he take his own salary?" Lutfi asked. "Yes," was the angry reply. "That's what they told me at the pay window for seasonal workers...."

"Maybe he's gone to do some shopping!"

"Before giving us our salaries?!"

"That's not out of the question. He does something new every day...."

They all looked furious. The director – an old fourth-grader* – frowned, and a short silence prevailed until Mustafa broke it with one of his laughs. "Just think," he said, "he might have been robbed in the street!"

Everyone laughed weakly, very weakly in fact; they sounded more like sighs of disapproval.

"Maybe he's had an accident!" Lutfi said. They all looked furious again, and so he corrected himself.

"Whatever happens to 'Uncle' Ibrahim involves the entire department...."

"Unless he's got a private cashier's office behind him!" said Ahmad angrily, hinting at Mustafa's rich wife.

Everyone gloated at that remark, but the director tapped on his desk with his Parker pen which he had been given on a happy occasion. He told the department to control itself, although he was really just covering up his own increasing anxiety.

"What happens to money in such circumstances?" the soldier asked in spite of everything.

"Exactly the same as in cases of theft." Nobody laughed.

"What would happen in case of an accident?" the soldier continued.

"Maybe he's been robbed in a crowd, or perhaps the police station is holding the money till things become clear. We'll all be dead and gone before you get it back!"

However, it was obvious that the reserves of laughter had dried up altogether. They all looked gloomy, and the passage of time seemed to weigh more heavily on them than illness itself. Someone asked what on earth had happened to make the day start so badly, and Ahmad started to look for 'Uncle' Ibrahim in the entire inspectorate. When he came back, his face made it clear that his efforts had

---

* i.e., a non-university graduate who has only reached this low administrative grade at such a late age in his life.

failed.

The director thought about the strange problem which had never occurred to anyone; he refused to believe it.. The stupid fool will appear at the door suddenly, he told himself, and will be greeted by a hail of abuse. He'll have all manner of excuses to offer. But....If not, what could be done? Lutfi had a rich wife, and Samir was known to be a rogue. But what about the other poor devils like Ahmad who might be finished by this disaster? The butter seller came back again, but did not have time even to open his mouth. "Wait!" the director yelled at him. "It's not the day of judgement yet; we're in a government department, not a sidewalk market...."

The man staggered back in confusion. Some of the civil servants from the inspectorate came to visit the department and look at the situation. Some of them thought about cracking a joke, but they found the atmosphere very melancholy and the jokes faded away before they even left their mouths. There was an air of anxiety and everyone stopped working.

"My heart tells me," said Ahmad with a sigh, "that it's already happened! We're doomed, friends!..." Then he got up. "I'll go and ask the doorman of the ministry about him," he said.

He disappeared in a rush. After a while he came back. "The doorman confirms," he yelled angrily, "that he saw him leaving the ministry around nine o'clock this morning!" He carried on in a strangled tone of voice. "What an utter calamity! He can't sell his whole life for a hundred and fifty or two hundred pounds! Could be an accident! Who knows?! Lord in heaven above, this month will never end!"

Lutfi sensed that some of them were looking at him from time to time. "A terrible catastrophe," he said in distress. "Some of you may be wondering how it concerns me! The truth is that my rich wife doesn't pay out a single millieme of her own money."

Ten curses were heaped upon him in secret, but none looked at him.

"Can you believe it, for heaven's sake?" said Ahmad with a sigh. "By the one and only God, I swear to you that after the second day of each month I come and go without a single millieme in my pocket. No coffee, no tea, no cigarettes. I have to walk; there's no way I can use any kind of transportation. Children at secondary school, children at university; and heavy debt because of medicine. God in heaven, what can I do?!"

When it passed one o'clock, the director stood up with a worried look on his face and left his desk. "I must report this to the general supervisor," he said.

The general supervisor listened to the story with evident annoyance. "Isn't it possible he'll come back," he asked, "whatever you may be thinking?"

"I've really completely despaired of that. It's getting on toward two o'clock...."

"You know of course," said the general supervisor in a critical tone, "that your conduct is at fault and contrary to instructions...."

The director cowered in a despairing silence. "All the departments do it...." he muttered.

"So what! Two wrongs don't make a right. Write me a memorandum so that I can submit it to the deputy minister...."

The director cringed. "Everyone needs his salary badly," he said. "We've never had anything like this happen before...."

"What do you want me to do?"

"We haven't received our salaries and haven't signed the list...."

The silence thickened. The director looked like a lost man. The general supervisor lost patience with him and started busying himself with the papers on his desk. The director now relinquished his position and proceeded towards the door with very heavy footsteps. Before reaching the door, he heard the supervisor's voice. "Infom the police...." he was told harshly.

The secretarial department went down to the police station, and made their way to the officer's room between a lot of women sitting cross-legged on the floor. In front of them was a group of brawling men with blood stained clothes being led along by a policeman. Behind a locked door screams of pain and cries for help could be heard. Mr. Kamil told the officer the story from beginning to end. He told him that 'Uncle' Ibrahim was the office boy; he was fifty-five years old and had started in the printing house, but had been made an office boy when he was rude to his boss. His basic salary was six pounds. The civil servants told the officer that he was a good man although he was eccentric and would seem a little distracted at times; he would talk to you, join in a conversation which had nothing whatever to do with him, or volunteer some general observations about politics totally out of context. All they could say about his home was that he lived in house 111 in Darb al-Halla. He had never stolen before or done anything which would lead you to doubt his integrity. After completing the report, the officer said that the station would first make sure that he was not an accident victim, and then the investigation would take its course. The civil servants saw there was nothing to do but to leave. As they came out of the station, they looked almost drunk in their confusion. They were all talking at once, and kept trading complaints and questions about what they could do about the awful responsibility waiting for them at home. They were all united by a corporate desire to remain together till they could find a solution to their problem but in the end they were forced to separate and go to their own homes. The director returned home with no hope of anything but a poker game. Mustafa, who worked on the typewriter, made for the loan places in Bab ash-Sha'riyya where he used to go in times of crisis to borrow money at exorbitant rates. Lutfi's wife used to take charge of the household expenses but he had to devise some way of

get-ting his monthly pocket money out of her. The soldier –
who was a young bachelor living under his father's wing –
decided to tell his father to accept him for this month as
though he were still a schoolboy. Hammam's wife was a
part of a savings association with her neighbors, and he
would have to convince her to ask for her share which had
been set aside for clothes so that he could spend it on household matters, regardless of the cursing, argument and tears
which would inevitably be involved. Things were relatively
easy for Samir; as soon as he was left on his own, he
thought, he would really be in a fix with no way out, if it
were not for bribery. There remained Ahmad the archive
clerk. His friends really wondered if he'd be able to survive.
He wandered along the road without paying the slightest
attention to the people or vehicles around him. He went into his house with a sigh; he looked very ashen as he threw
himself down on the first chair and closed his eyes. His wife
came in bringing the kitchen smells with her. "What's the
matter with you?" she asked in consternation.

"We won't be getting any salary this month!" he said
without any preliminaries.

"Why not, for God's sake?!" she asked in amazement.
'Uncle' Ibrahim brought your salary round early this
morning!"

He leapt to his feet like a drowning man who finds that
he is breathing at long last. Meanwhile, his wife went out
and came back with a wad of notes, his complete monthly
salary! He was so happy, he felt almost crazy. He stretched
out his hands. "God be good to you, 'Uncle' Ibrahim...may
He comfort you, 'Uncle' Ibrahim...."

The police raided 'Uncle' Ibrahim's house in Darb al-
Halla. It consisted of a ground-floor room on the courtyard
of an old house with walls almost in a state of collapse. All
there was in the room was a shabby mattress, a mat, a stove,
a cooking pot, a teak tray, and a one-eyed old woman who
was obviously his wife. When she was questioned about her
husband, she replied that he was at the ministry. She then

declared that she knew nothing about his disappearance; he had no clothes except for a *gallabiyya*,* so they searched it and found a small piece of *hashish*. They took the woman to the police station, She said she knew nothing about his running away, nor about the theft of which he was being accused. She wept and cursed for a long time and then started talking about their life together. At first, she said, he had been a good husband and they had had children. One of them was working in the Canal area, and they had lost touch with him for some years; another had been killed in a tram accident when he was ten; and their daughter had married a building worker who had taken her to live in the limits of Upper Egypt, and so she had vanished from their lives just like her brother at the Canal. She admitted that 'Uncle' Ibrahim had changed noticeably in recent months after reaching the age of discretion. She had heard rumours that he had become attached to a lottery-ticket seller** at Fuad's cafe, and these rumours had caused a serious row between them in the full view of the neighborhood of Darb al-Halla.

The detectives raided Fuad's cafe and came back with a strange collection of children and adolescent cigarette-butt collectors and some shoe cleaners. They all remembered 'Uncle' Ibrahim when he was described to them. They said that in recent months he had sat on the furthest chair in the passage which branched off from the main street sipping coffee and staring at the English girl! It emerged that by English girl they meant the lottery-ticket seller, who was seventeen years old with blonde hair and blue eyes; she had been a cigarette-butt collector originally too, and nearly all of them admitted having some personal relationship with her and that the same had been the case with some of the good and modest folk who visited the cafe!! 'Uncle' Ibrahim cared a great deal for her. He had seen her once as he was

* robe
** A hint that the seller is also a prostitute.

crossing the street, and, when he found out that she was one of the regular features of Fuad's cafe, he had started sitting on a chair at the end of the passageway every evening so that he could see her. He would call her over quite openly to buy a lottery-ticket from her and, if the truth were told, to keep her there as long as possible. From the very first, the girl realized that he was infatuated with her and told them all about it. They started spying on him day after day and regarded him as an enormous joke; he meanwhile was so infatuated with her that he was totally unaware of them. One day, she told them all that he wanted to marry her! He would give her a happy life, she claimed, without all the worries of hard work and vagrancy. They laughed for ages; they looked on the whole thing as a joke, on the one hand because the thought of marriage had never occurred to them, and on the other because the man in question seemed the least likely of all to fit the picture of the bridegroom as they conceived him.

"He looks like one of us!" one of them said with a scoff.

"He's a rich man...." she replied proudly.

They all laughed once more. However, the girl stopped coming to the cafe and vanished from their thoughts altogether!

Generally speaking, the police were convinced they had a lead, but they didn't know that the other end of it was in Abuqir, the suburb of Alexandria. Yes, 'Uncle' Ibrahim was in Abuqir. He was sitting relaxed on the beach looking alternately at the sea and at Yasmina* whose golden hair was flying in the breeze. He had shaved, and his bald head was covered by a skullcap as white as milk which reflected his blooming complexion. Yasmina was wearing an elegant dress, and her fresh complexion gleamed like distilled water. It was a happy, contented, peaceful family scene, even though there was a cold nip in the April wind. The place was almost empty; none of the summer visitors had arrived yet. The

* Meaning 'jasmine'.

Greek house owners were far from the beach.. Love was hovering and dancing round the beautiful scene; Ibrahim's eyes had a look of anticipation and amazement about them, as though he were seeing the world for the first time with all the innocence of childhood. He'd never seen any sea before; in fact, he'd never been out of Cairo all his life. So the roaring sea, the expanse of shore and the blue sky dotted with white clouds, all this delighted him as it wafted through his mind. He began listening to the intermittent roar of the sea with a happy smile which never left his lips. It seemed that he was rid of the snares of anxiety and floating around in a kind of dream; he was obviously enjoying the touching melodies of love which his besotted heart was playing over and over again.

The girl was stretched out in front of him. She seemed relaxed, but a somnolent silence encompassed her and weighed down her eyelids in a way which suggested that she was bored. It was Mr. Lutfi in the secretarial department who had told him about Abuqir quite by chance. Lutfi would spend the summer at this resort every year, and, before he went and when he came back, he would tell his colleagues how beautiful and peaceful it was and what marvellous fish there were there. 'Uncle' Ibrahim's imagination was full of the idea of a summer resort, and finally he had worked out a way to get there. He had come equipped with clothes, make-up implements, presents and things for all kinds of mood, such as *hashish* which would be needed on a honeymoon. The whole day was spent between the furnished room he had taken and the sea shore. His only preoccupations were to love, look around him, smoke, eat, drink and talk. In one week, he managed to spend more than he had ever spent in a whole year. His sweetheart never stopped asking for things, and he was always ready to answer as quick as a flash. She had eccentric tastes, even wine and drugs; she was very blatant about it almost to the point of being a nuisance. "Where do you get the money?" she asked him once.

"I'm a local dignitary!...." he replied with a laugh. The wine could be seen in the coloring of her face.

"I understand...." she said suspiciously. "God forgive you...!"

"You've only got four teeth," she said laughing simply. "One on top and three below...!"

He laughed indulgently. Sometimes he felt worried, but he was determined to be happy; and he knew more than anyone how fleeting that happiness could be. All he hoped for was to preserve the happiness he had got up till now and not be arrested till the pillars of this happiness collapsed naturally when he had spent the last millieme he had. This was why he decided to be happy even though his sweetheart seemed to be grumbling a lot. She was dying to see Alexandria, but he refused adamantly.

"I told you I understood!" she said with a cunning which she inherited from the pavements.

His answer was to buy her a lovely bracelet and put in front of her fruit, drink and the forbidden cigarettes. He kissed her rosy cheek and smiling lovingly at her. "Look at the sea and the sky," he said. "Be happy with what you've got, and have a good time!"

He wanted her to be happy like himself. Before he had left, he had gone round with his head lowered; all he had seen of the world was dirt and dust, or else his own preoccupations and worries. But now here he was seeing things he had never seen before; the dawn as it rose magically, the sunset with its incredible colors pouring out at twilight, the ever-watchful stars, the gleaming moon and the horizon stretching away to infinity. All this he saw through the creative power of love till he wondered whether there could be any hardship after all this....

At the beginning of June, the first family which had come for an early summer holiday appeared on the beach. 'Uncle' Ibrahim's heart leapt and he felt that adversity was approaching like Fate; soon his happiness would vanish, and forever. This made him even more determined to enjoy the happiness he had been given and so he started chain-smoking *hashish*. One day, he was at the grocer's and spotted Mr. Lutfi, the civil servant in the secretarial department, at the end of the street with a real estate agent. 'Uncle' Ibrahim panicked, dashed over to a side alley and then slunk away back to his room. Lutfi had come to hire a house for the two months of July and August as he usually did for the summer. It would be just a few weeks before he would be wandering far and wide along the seashore and then there would be no place left for 'Uncle' Ibrahim. The hand of fate was rapping on his door and he could not find any place for himself. His lovely dream would vanish just like those scudding clouds. His sweetheart would desert him just like his own sighs; he still loved her in spite of her moans, her temper and her peppery tongue. Yes, he loved her and thanked her for the happiness she had given him and the spirit of youth she had breathed into him. So God forgive her and make her happy! He found himself alone in his room. He began counting the money he had left and then wrapped it around his chest. He heard a movement at the door. He turned around and saw her coming towards him. He asked himself whether she had seen him and read a cunning look in her eyes. For that very reason, he could not get to sleep when he threw himself down beside her in bed. He spent the night wide awake thinking. From deep down inside him, he heard a tender voice telling him to give her the money and set her free. I've still got some time left, he said, to which the voice replied that he should give her the money and let her go. The lovely, homeless little girl. Who had her father been...and her mother?

"I haven't got anyone in the world...." she'd said once candidly.

That's the way it was with him too. He felt something like a snake touching him in the dark. He focused his attention on her thieving little hand; she was trying to rob him. Was that why the cunning little devil had tried to exhaust him so that he would be fast asleep! The devil. He grabbed her hand and she let out a groan in the darkness. Then there was silence.

"Why?" he asked bitterly. "When did I ever refuse to give you anything?"

She pounced on his hand and bit it viciously till he yelled and pushed her away forcefully. It was the first harsh gesture he had ever made towards her. He leapt for the light and put it on. He looked first at his wrist which was splattered with blood. "How can a little girl like you be so wicked!" he asked.

For a moment she looked ashamed and then turned her back on him.

"How could you try to steal your own money?" She frowned furiously but did not say a word. "I didn't want any more than I had...." he resumed, and then with a bitter laugh "God forgive you!"

Next morning, he gave her most of the money that was left, packed up her things and took her to the station.

From then on Abuqir seemed bleak. Things changed slowly and the summer holiday-makers came up in throngs. He moved to Alexandria where he could wander unconcerned on his own. Once he found himself in front of the Abu l-Abbas mosque and went in. He prayed two prayers as a salute to the mosque and then sat with his face turned towards the wall. He was feeling desperately sad and de-spondent. He prayed to his Lord in a whisper. "You can't be happy with what has happened to me or with what is hap-pening everywhere. A girl so small, lovely and evil; does that please you?! Where are my children? Does that please you? The world is after me merely because I love you; does that please you? Among millions of people, I feel so alone, it almost kills me; does that please you?" He burst into tears. As he was leaving the mosque, a voice startled him. "'Uncle' Ibrahim!" it shouted. He turned round in aston-ishment without any will to resist, and saw a huge man coming towards him with a look of triumphant satisfaction on his face. From his appearance, he realized detective. He stayed where he was in resignation. The man grabbed him by the shoulder. "You've worn us all out looking for you, damn you...."

The detective noticed that 'Uncle Ibrahim had resigned himself to his fate as he was leading him along and looked red about the eyes. "Can you tell me what made you do all that at your age?!" he asked.

"God...." he muttered with a smile, and then raised his finger up to the sky.

The word escaped from him like a sigh....

The Happy Man

He woke up in the morning and discovered that he was happy. "What's this?" he asked himself. He could not think of any word which described his state of mind more accurately and precisely than 'happy'. This was distinctly peculiar when compared with the state he was usually in when he woke up. He would be half-asleep from staying so late at the newspaper office. He would face life with a sense of strain and contemplation. Then he would get up, whetting his determination to face up to all inconveniences and withstand all difficulties.

Today he felt happy, full of happiness as a matter of fact. There was no arguing about it. The symptoms were quite clear and their vigour and obviousness were such as to impose themselves on his senses and mind all at once. Yes, indeed; he was happy. If this was not happiness, then what was? He felt that his limbs were well proportioned and func-tioning perfectly. They were working in superb harmony with each other and with the world around him. Inside him, he felt a boundless power, an imperishable energy, an ability to achieve anything with confidence, precision, and obvious success. His heart was overflowing with love for people, animals and things, and with an all-engulfing sense of optimism and joy. It was as if he were no longer troubled or bothered by fear, anxiety, sickness, death, argument, or the question of earning a living. Even more important than that, and something he could not analyze, it was a feeling which penetrated to every cell of his body and soul, it played a tune full of delight, pleasure, serenity and peace, and hummed in its incredible melodies the whispering sound of the world which is denied to the unhappy.

He felt drunk with ecstasy and savoured it slowly with a feeling of surprise. He asked himself where it had come from and how; the past provided no explanation and the future could not justify it. Where did it come from, then, and how?! How long would it last? Would it stay with him till breakfast? Would it give him enough time to get to the newspaper office? Just a minute though, he thought...it won't last because it can't. If it did, man would be turned into an angel or something even higher. So he told himself that he should devote his attention to savouring it, living with it, and storing up its nectar before it became a mere memory with no way of proving it or even being sure that it had ever existed.

He ate his breakfast with a relish, and this time nothing distracted his attention while he was eating. He gave 'Uncle' Bashir who was waiting on him such a beaming smile that the poor man felt rather alarmed and taken aback. Usually he would only look in his direction to give orders or ask questions; although, on most occasions, he treated him fairly well.

"Tell me, 'Uncle' Bashir," he asked the servant, "am I a happy man?"

The poor man was startled. He realized why his servant was confused; for the first time ever he was talking to him as a colleague or friend. He encouraged his servant to forget about his worries and asked him with unusual insistence to answer his question.

"Through God's grace and favour, you are happy," the servant replied.

"You mean, I should be happy. Anyone with my job, living in my house, and enjoying my health, should be happy. That's what you want to say. But do you think I'm really happy?"

The servant replied, "You work too hard, Sir," after yet more insistence, "it's more than any man can stand...."

He hesitated, but his master gestured to him to continue with what he had to say.

"You get angry a lot," he said, "and have fierce arguments with your neighbors...."

He interrupted him by laughing loudly. "What about you," he asked, "don't you have any worries?"

"Of course, no man can be free of worry."

"You mean that complete happiness is an impossible quest?"

"That applies to life in general...."

How could he have dreamed up this incredible happiness? He or any other human being? It was a strange, unique happiness, as though it were a private secret he had been given. In the meeting hall of the newspaper building, he spotted his main rival in this world sitting down thumbing through a magazine. The man heard his footsteps, but did not look up from the magazine. He had undoubtedly noticed him in some way and was therefore pretending to ignore him so as to keep his own peace of mind. At.some circulation meetings, they would argue so violently with each other that sparks began to fly and they would exchange bitter words. One stage more, and they would come to blows. A week ago, his rival had won in the union elections and he had lost. He had felt pierced by a sharp, poisoned arrow, and the world had darkened before his eyes. Now here he was approaching his rival's seat; the sight of him sitting there did not make him excited, nor did the memories of their dispute spoil his composure. He approached him with a pure and carefree heart, feeling drunk with his incredible happiness; his face showed an expression full of tolerance and forgiveness. It was as though he were approaching some other man towards whom he had never had any feel-ings of enmity, or perhaps he might be renewing a friend-ship again. "Good morning!" he said without feeling any compunction.

The man looked up in amazement. He was silent for a few moments until he recovered, and then returned the greeting curtly. It was as though he did not believe his eyes and ears.

He sat down alongside the man. "Marvellous weather today...." he said.

"Okay...." the other replied guardedly.

"Weather to fill your heart with happiness."

His rival looked at him closely and cautiously. "I'm glad that you're so happy...." he muttered.

"Inconceivably happy...." he replied with a laugh.

"I hope," the man continued in a rather hesitant tone of voice, "that I shan't spoil your happiness at the meeting of the administrative council...."

"Not at all. My views are well known, but I don't mind if the members adopt your point of view. That won't spoil my happiness!"

"You've changed a great deal overnight," the man said with a smile.

"The fact is that I'm happy, inconceivably happy."

The man examined his face carefully. "I bet your dear son has changed his mind about staying in Canada?!" he asked.

"Never, never, my friend," he replied, laughing loudly. "He is still sticking to his decision...."

"But that was the principal reason for your being so sad...."

"Quite true. I've often begged him to come back out of pity for me in my loneliness and to serve his country. But he told me that he's going to open an engineering office with a Canadian partner; in fact, he's invited me to join him in it. Let him live where he'll be happy. I'm quite happy here – as you can see, inconceivably happy...."

The man still looked a little doubtful. "Quite extraordinarily brave!" he said.

"I don't know what it is, but I'm happy in the full meaning of the word."

Yes indeed, this was full happiness; full, firm, weighty, and vital. As deep as absolute power, widespread as the wind, fierce as fire, bewitching as scent, transcending nature. It could not possibly last.

The other man warmed to his display of affection. "The truth is," he said, "that I always picture you as someone with a fierce and violent temperament which causes him a good deal of trouble and leads him to trouble other people

"Really?"

"You don't know how to make a truce, you've no concept of intermediate solutions. You work with your nerves, with the marrow in your bones. You fight bitterly as though any problem is a matter of life and death!"

"Yes, that's true."

He accepted the criticism without any difficulty and with an open heart. His wave expanded into a boundless ocean of happiness. He struggled to control an innocent, happy laugh which the other man interpreted in a way far removed from its pure motives.

"So then," he asked, "you think it's necessary to be able to take a balanced view of events, do you?"

"Of course. I remember, by way of example, the argument we had the day before yesterday about racism. We both had the same views on the subject; it's something worth being zealous about, even to the point of anger. But what kind of anger? An intellectual anger, abstract to a certain extent; not the type which shatters your nerves, ruins your digestion, and gives you palpitations. Not so?"

"That's obvious; I quite understand...." He struggled to control a second laugh and succeeded. His heart refused to renounce one drop of its joy. Racism, Vietnam, Palestine,... no problem could assail that fortress of happiness which was encircling his heart. When he remembered a problem, his heart guffawed. He was happy. It was a tyrannical happiness, despising all misery and laughing at any hardship; it wanted to laugh, dance, sing, and distribute its spirit of laughter, dancing and singing among the various problems of the world.

He could not bear to stay in his office at the newspaper

he felt no desire to work at all. He hated the very idea of thinking about his daily business, and completely failed to bring his mind down from its stronghold in the kingdom of happiness. How could he possibly write about a trolley bus falling into the Nile when he was so intoxicated by this frightening happiness? Yes, it really was frightening. How could it be anything else, when there was no reason for it at all, when it was so strong that it made him exhausted and paralyzed his will; apart from the fact that it had been with him for half a day without letting up in the slightest degree?!

He left the pages of paper blank and started walking backwards and forwards across the room, laughing and cracking his fingers....

He felt slightly worried; it did not penetrate deep enough to spoil his happiness, but paused on the surface of his mind like an abstract idea. It occurred to him that he might recall the tragedies of his life so that he could test their effect on his happiness. Perhaps they would be able to bring back some idea of balance or security, at least until his happiness began to flag a little. For example, he remembered his wife's death in all its various aspects and details. What had happened? The event appeared to him as a series of movements without any meaning or effect, as though it had happened to some other woman, the wife of another man, in some distant historical age. In fact, it had a contagious effect which prompted a smile, and then even provoked laughter. He could not stop himself laughing, and there he was guffawing, ha...ha...ha!

The same thing happened when he remembered the first letter his son had sent him saying that he wanted to emigrate to Canada. The sound of his guffaws as he paraded the bloody tragedies of the world before him would have attracted the attention of the newspaper workers and passersby in the street, had it not been for the thickness of the walls. He could do nothing to dislodge his happiness. Memories of unhappy times hit him like waves being sandy beach under the golden rays of the sun.

He excused himself from attending the administrative council and left the newspaper office without writing a word. After lunch, he lay down on his bed as usual but could not sleep. In fact, sleep seemed an impossibility to him. Nothing gave him any indication that it was coming, even slowly. He was in a place alight and gleaming, resounding with sleeplessness and joy. He had to calm down and relax, to quieten his senses and limbs, but how could he do it? He gave up trying to sleep, and got up. He began to hum as he was walking around his house. If this keeps up he told himself, I won't be able to sleep, just as I can't work or feel sad. It was almost time for him to go to the club, but he did not feel like meeting any friends. What was the point of exchanging views on public affairs and private worries?! What would they think if they found him laughing at every major problem? What would they say? How would they picture things? How would they explain it? No, he did not need anyone, nor did he want to spend the evening talking. He should be by himself, and go for a long walk to get rid of some of his excess vitality and think about his situation. What had happened to him? How was it that this incredible happiness had overwhelmed him? How long would he have to carry it on his shoulders? Would it keep depriving him of work, friends, sleep and peace of mind?! Should he resign himself to it? Should he abandon himself to the flood to play with him as the whim took it? Or should he look for a way out for himself through thought, action, or advice?

◆ ◆ ◆ ◆

When he was called into the examination room in the clinic of his friend, the specialist in internal medicine, he felt a little alarmed. The doctor looked at him with a smile. "You don't look like someone who's complaining about being ill," he said.

"I haven't come to see you because I'm ill " he told the doctor in a hesitant tone of voice, "but because I'm happy!"

The doctor looked piercingly at him with a questioning air.

"Yes," he repeated to underline what he had said, "because I'm happy!"

There was a period of silence. On one side, there was anxiety, and on the other, questioning and amazement.

"It's an incredible feeling which can't be defined in any other way, but it's very serious...."

The doctor laughed. "I wish your illness was contagious," he said, prodding him jokingly.

"Don't treat it as a joke. It's very serious, as I told you. I'll describe it to you...."

He told him all about his happiness from the time he had woken up in the morning till he had felt compelled to visit him.

"Haven't you been taking drugs, alcohol, or tranquillizers?"

"Absolutely nothing like that."

"Have you had some success in an important sphere of your life; work...love...money?"

"Nothing like that either. I've twice as much to worry about as I have to make me feel glad...."

"Perhaps if you were patient for a while...."

"I've been patient all day. I'm afraid I'll be spending the night wandering around...."

The doctor gave him a precise, careful, and comprehensive examination and then shrugged his shoulders in despair. "You're a picture of health," he said.

"And so?"

"I could advise you to take a sleeping pill, but it would be better if you consulted a nerve specialist...."

The examination was repeated in the nerve specialist's clinic with the selfsame precision, care, and comprehensiveness. "Your nerves are sound," the doctor told him, "they're in enviable condition!"

"Haven't you got a plausible explanation for my condition?" he asked hopefully.

"Consult a gland specialist!" the doctor replied, shaking his head.

The examination was conducted for a third time in the gland specialist's clinic with the same precision, care and comprehensiveness. "I congratulate you!" the doctor told him. "Your glands are in good condition.

He laughed. He apologized for laughing, laughing as he did so. Laughter was his way of expressing his alarm and despair.

He left the clinic with the feeling that he was alone; alone in the hands of his tyrannical happiness with no helper, no guide and no friend. Suddenly, he remembered the doctor's sign he sometimes saw from the window of his office in the newspaper building. It was true that he had no confidence in psychiatrists even though he had read about the significance of psychoanalysis. Apart from that, he knew that their tentacles were very long and they kept their patients tied in a sort of long association. He laughed as he remembered the method of cure through free association and the problems which it eventually uncovers. He was laughing as his feet carried him towards the psychiatrist's clinic, and imagined the doctor listening to his incredible complaints about feeling happy, when he was used to hearing people complain about hysteria, schizophrenia, anxiety, and so on.

"The truth is, Doctor, that I've come to see you because I'm happy!"

He looked at the doctor to see what effect his statement had had on him, but noticed that he was keeping his composure. He felt ridiculous. "I'm inconceivably happy...." he said in a tone of confidence.

He began to tell the doctor his story, but the latter stopped him with a gesture of his hand. "An overwhelming, incredible, debilitating happiness?" he asked quietly.

He stared at him in amazement and was on the point of saying something, but the doctor spoke first. "A happiness which has made you stop working," he asked, "abandon your friends, and detest going to sleep....?"

"You're a miracle!" he shouted.

"Every time you get involved in some misfortune," the psychiatrist continued quietly, "you dissolve into laughter...?"

"Sir...are you familiar with the invisible?"

"No!" he said with a smile, "nothing like that. But I get a similar case in my clinic at least once a week!"

"Is it an epidemic?" he asked.

"I didn't say that, and I wouldn't claim that it's been possible to analyze one case into its primary elements as yet."

"But is it a disease?"

"All the cases are still under treatment."

"But are you satisfied without any doubt that they aren't natural cases...?"

"That's a necessary assumption for the job; there's only...."

"Have you noticed any of them to be deranged in...." he asked anxiously, pointing to his head.

"Absolutely not," the doctor replied convincingly. "I assure you that they're all intelligent in every sense of the word...."

The doctor thought for a moment. "We should have two sessions a week, I think?" he said.

"Very well...." he replied in resignation.

"There's no sense in getting alarmed or feeling sad...."

Alarmed, sad? He smiled, and his smile kept on getting broader. A laugh slipped out, and before long, he was dissolving into laughter. He was determined to control himself, but his resistance collapsed completely. He started guffawing loudly...

A Photograph

Abd al-Mutallib proceeded with his breakfast which consisted of a piece of sour cheese, some baked bread and a cup of coffee. Opposite him sat his wife with her head buried in the newspaper. The whole apartment exuded an air of quiet like old age itself. It was always like that except for visiting days, and they were kept alive by their sons. The woman pulled the paper closer to her eyes in a gesture of sudden shock, but he looked at her unconcernedly. His concern was rarely aroused ever since he had been pensioned off.

"Poor girl!" the woman muttered sadly.

"It's always the accidents page or the obituaries!" he told himself.

She handed him the paper. "Young girl, pretty too...." she said regretfully, "look...."

"Good God!" A body stretched out on the sand. Clear cut features and youthful appearance; eyes shut forever. He looked at the newspaper without taking it from her.

"Murdered?" he asked.

"In the desert behind the Pyramid. Back of her head smashed in. Nothing stolen from her. Unidentified."

"Same old story," he said chewing a mouthful.

"But nothing was stolen!"

"Love, bad luck, anything. It stands to reason she wasn't killed for nothing. "

"She was beautiful. How young the poor girl was!" She looked closely at the photograph. "Her poor mother!" she said. She put the paper down on the table. "I really wonder," she continued," how anybody can murder another human being!"

"You've lived through two world wars and scores of local wars; don't forget that."

"War's something else. It's not like killing someone face to face; with motive, with cunning, bitterness. I'm sure the poor girl felt quite safe going with him...."

"Damn it. And why did she go with him?"

"God knows," she said with a sigh, "and He is forgiving."

♦ ♦ ♦ ♦

In an apartment in building 50 in Shubra, a young girl was looking in amazement at the photograph of the murdered girl; she could hardly believe her eyes. She rushed over to her mother with the paper.

"Mother, look!...." she yelled. Her mother looked at the photograph and read the story, then looked up inquiringly at her daughter.

"Shalabiyya, Mother," the girl said emotionally, "don't you remember her?"

The woman looked closely at the photograph and then her eyes opened wide in astonishment and shock. "Good Lord," she shouted, "it is Shalabiyya; you're right."

"She stayed with us five years ago," the girl said regretfully.

"Yes, that's right. I wonder how and why she was murdered?!"

The mother muttered something unintelligible, but the girl was still upset. "She was a good girl, Mother; she would take orders patiently and with a smile. She used to sing folk songs in the bath with a lovely, innocent voice...." And she added in a somewhat reproachful tone: –"We dismissed her for no reason at all!"

"She's a poor, wretched girl – God have mercy on her – but we didn't do her any wrong...."

"She was kind, innocent, and polite; I don't know why

she was thrown out...."

"She wasn't thrown out without good reason," her mother said indignantly. "It was all fated anyway."

"Maybe if she'd stayed with us...." the girl said with a sigh.

"You're crazy!" her mother interrupted angrily. "Everything depends on God's will, doesn't it?"

"Poor girl," she said with her voice lowered. "I used to love her, and Father never wanted to throw her out...."

Her mother frowned at the mention of the word 'Father' and her eyes seemed to cloud over with disturbing mem-ories. "Enough" she said in a dry voice. "God have mercy on her, and that's enough...."

The mother looked at the photograph once more. "She wasn't dressed in servant's clothes...." she muttered.

"Perhaps...."

"Whatever the reason may have been, I did her no wrong," her mother interrupted. "God have mercy on her...."

Silence prevailed.

"The police are asking anyone who recognizes the photograph to come forward and give their information," the girl said.

"We've had no contact with her for five years," her mother said firmly. "We can't help the investigation in any way, and, in any case, you've no idea of the trouble anyone who goes to the police will have to go through."

Thereupon she threw the paper out of the way. "Good God, what a morning!" she said.

♦ ♦ ♦ ♦

Mr. Anwar Hamid noticed the photograph as he was thumbing through the paper during a short break in his work at the inspection department. He stared at it with such a shock that his colleague in the office noticed.

"Good news, I hope?" he asked.

"A friend just died," he replied, folding the paper and keeping control of himself. But he continued to feel upset; it plagued him all the time. Shalabiyya, the girl who worked in the workshop, the beautiful virgin, who he was eventually forced to marry as a common-law wife. He had made it a condition against his own better judgement that she should carry on working. When she became pregnant, he extracted an agreement from her that she would get an abortion.

"You don't really love me," she had said. "You don't think of me as your wife."

"Of course, you're my wife," he had said gently, "but I don't want any heirs!"

When, in the period that followed, life became unbearable, he made up his mind and let her go. His friend Abid, the chief accountant, had witnessed the whole thing and kept quiet about it. He felt so upset that he went into his friend's office and showed him the photograph.

"Poor girl," the latter muttered, "I wonder how she was killed."

"We'll know tomorrow or the day after. It's not difficult to guess."

They exchanged glances, and Anwar Hamid wasn't too happy about it.

"She was very stubborn," he said. "What could I do?"

"She loved you very much," the director replied in a softened tone of voice, " and she wanted to be a mother...."

"But people, the family!...you know that very well,"

"Of course. God forgive us all!"

For a moment, he was angry. "Shall I go to the police?" he asked.

"I should think so," the director replied.

"But won't that cause problems when I'm about to get married?"

"Don't go then," the director replied after thinking for a while. "If your name comes up in the investigation in the future, say you didn't see the photograph."

♦ ♦ ♦ ♦

Hasuna al-Maghribi did not see the photograph till the
afternoon which was the time when he usually woke up.
He rubbed his eyes in disbelief. "Durriyya," he said, "to the
Devil!" He looked at the photograph for a while. "Why was
she murdered?!" he murmured.

He went into the bathroom and belched up the acidity of
the alcohol. He soon felt calm again. "You're a crooked
devil!" he said.

He began to wash his face. "The penalty fits the kind of
work," he continued. He started to shave. "I knew you
when you were divorced and in very poor circumstances,"
he said as though he were talking to his own image in the
mirror. "That was after you'd tried out middle-class moral-
ity. I gave you love and made you a star in this house. The
finest people in town adored you. And how did you repay
me? By running away. Yes, you ran away to be murdered in
the desert. So to Hell with you...."

At about nine in the evening, the men came and sat
down round the gambling table. Inayat and Bahija moved
round with the whiskey and relishes. They had all heard the
news.

"You may be called to the investigation, Hasuna...."

"I haven't see her for a year," he replied disdainfully.

"Even so...."

"It would be wise," said Sa'id al-Imam cautiously, "not
to go till they arrest the murderer...."

"I had nothing to do with the crime...." yelled Hasuna
anxiously.

"Go to the police," said Husni al-Dinari, "and tell them
all you know...."

"Do you want me to confess that she worked here?" the
man asked in bewilderment.

"No, no! Merely say that she was your friend and that
you haven't seen her for a year...."

"And what if they ask me about my job...my identification card...or enquire about where I live?!"

"There's even more danger in saying nothing at all...."

He gestured angrily with his hand. "She had to be murdered, didn't she," he yelled, "just so as to make a mess of my life!?"

"I gave you enough advice!" the man retorted angrily, "but you treated her very badly, even though she loved you to distraction...."

♦ ♦ ♦ ♦

Fathiyya as-Sultani woke up at around sunset in the room she shared with Dawlat, Ni'mat, Anisa and Aliyya. Durriyya (Shalabiyya) was the first thing that occurred to her. A volcano of anger erupted inside her and it did not leave her all the time she was in the bath while she was freshening herself up and standing in front of the mirror putting on her make-up. "Bloody bitch!" she exclaimed, "who does she think she is?"

Dawlat yawned; she realized to whom Fathiyya was referring. "She was drunk!" she said as though making excuses for Durriyya.

"What of it? She could drink a barrel full without feeling a thing." She forgot the subject for a few minutes while she combed her recalcitrant hair into place. "She looked at people above her class!" she said after a while. "Excuse me, my lady! Have you forgotten your throne on the back of a cow?"

"She was drunk," Ni'mat said. "That was unusual. She only wanted to make fun of you. I wonder where she spent the night?"

"Go to Hell! Tonight she'll find out who I am."

At the beginning of the evening she wandered along the Kornish for quite a while without any success. Then she made for the cake shop *Star of the East* and took her usual seat on the second floor; she started looking at the people there and waiting. From time to time, she would look towards the entrance poised and ready to greet her arch rival.

"Haven't you seen Durriya?" she asked the waiter when he went by.

"She'll be coming soon...." he replied without stopping.

♦ ♦ ♦ ♦

Adil spent the day dawdling in the gardens on the banks of the Nile and did not go to the University. He had not slept at all the previous night. He had the newspaper under his arm, and every time he found himself in a wilderness, he opened the accident page and looked at the photograph. He told himself that eventually he would drop with this tremendous fatigue. His spittle was dry and bitter, he told himself, and his breathing was slow. And now the raging hurricane had subsided, the wagging tongues had stopped and the plan had been carried out. Even so, he did not feel he had achieved any goal or seen hope fulfilled. Nothing, emptiness, downfall; predestined, with no way out. If it was risky to stay around, it was even worse to.run away. Where could he run to? How many people might have seen him taking her away? It seemed to him that some voice was calling him on the gradient up to the Pyramid, and apart from all that, the police seemed to be filling all the locked places like the wind.

"Where are you taking me?"

"It would be nice to go far into the desert."

"They are asking for you in college and waiting for you around the house. How impossible it is for us to move backwards for just one minute.

"Durriyya...you're always lying!"

"I never lie, but you don't believe me."

"I've loved you with all my heart, but you haven't got a heart."

"It's very dark here...."

"You're as hard as stone...."

"Adil...your voice sounds different...I don't like the dark."

"From now on, that's all you'll see...."

Everything is over. Now, here you are torturing me from your grave just as you did when you were alive. You were not a woman, you were not even human. Your heart never beat with love. You were an evil force created from evil to practice evil.

An Extraordinary Official

I was looking through the daily newspapers as I usually do every morning when I start work. The door opened without a knock and a strange man came in. His height and general size gave him an imposing appearance; he was wearing a good suit, and his tall, dark tarbush emphasized the pale complexion of his face. There was a certain distinction about him, and this was underlined by the dark glasses he wore and the thick square moustache of grey hair on his upper lip. He was in his sixties or thereabouts, but he strode into my office with a good deal of energy and vigor. He was car-rying an ivory-handled fly whisk in his right hand.

"Good morning," he said in a coarse voice. "Is this the press office?"

"Yes," I replied, although I'd hardly recovered from his abrupt intrusion. "Good morning!"

"I think it's under the Minister's office, isn't it?"

"Yes."

He brought out his wallet and took out a card which he handed to me. I looked at it and read: Ismail Bey al-Bajuri, Counsellor to the Prime Minister.

The words 'Prime Minister' exploded inside me. I had only been at my job for a year or a few months less. I stood up respectfully and smiled apologetically "Please sit down, Sir," I said, showing obvious signs of being flustered, "I'm at your service!"

But he walked hurriedly into the small elongated room till he was standing by the window at the far end looking out over the Al-Azhar Square. Then he came back to my desk. "Isn't the Minister here yet?" he asked.

"The Minister comes at about ten."

"What about the Director of his office?"

"The Director gets here at about nine...." He turned to one side so as to express his exasperation more easily, and then stretched out his hand to the in-tray. He looked through the files quickly. "Lots of columns haven't been filled out," he said, "and there's a complaint here which hasn't been answered for twenty days.!"

My heart sank. I asked myself what had happened to make the day start off so badly. "I distribute the complaints which are published in the newspapers to the appropriate department," I said. "They are the ones who hold things up...."

"Then why don't you hurry them up?"

"I do, of course. But some replies have to be submitted to the supervisory bodies in the provinces."

He shook his head in exasperation and then gestured at the door. "Follow me, please," he said in a commanding tone.

He walked through all the rooms in the ministry; I walk-ed alongside him although I stayed a pace behind him out of politeness. We went from one room to another until event-ually we started to return to my office. All the way, he kept scattering comments and observations around.

"Empty offices," he would say. "Where are the civil servants who should be in them now? What are all these bags stuffed full of papers? What's all this garbage doing here? And these piles of folders like so many tombs! And what a stench of oil and onions! Good heavens...."

I shook my head and smiled sadly to show how sorry I was. All the while, I was asking God to bring the day to a happy end.

"Everything's out of place!" he said. "If only the Prime Minister knew about it!"

We returned to my office and I stood behind my desk. He threw himself down on the couch in almost a reclining position and crossed one leg over the other knee. He clearly felt sorry for me in my confusion. "Sit down," he said.

So I sat. I felt somewhat encouraged by the gentle tone I detected in his coarse voice. He started looking me over in a desultory fashion from behind his dark glasses. "Are you from the university?" he asked me.

"Yes..."

"Why did you become a civil servant?"

I didn't answer.

"Say: 'To live!'", he replied for me. "All of us need to live, but life doesn't work out as it should!"

I lowered my head in agreement. At that moment I would have liked nothing so much as for the Director of the office of the Minister to appear and rescue me from my horrible predicament.

"I've been told to make a thorough investigation," he said. "It's a hard job, but, I ask myself, is there any point?"

I was surprised that he even deigned to reveal his important assignment to me, and at the same time I began to feel even more confused. "If you do it," I said, "it's bound to work out well!"

To my surprise, he yawned. There was an unsettling silence. He seemed very important; maybe the silence and waiting bothered him. He started talking, but this time, it seemed it was to himself: – "Man should look for peace of mind, but how can he get it?"

I wasn't sure whether it was safe to join in the conversation. "May the Lord give you good health, Sir," I said.

He uncrossed his legs. "Good health! What's that? It means complete equilibrium, conformity, and cooperation in any living unit. But there's small chance of realizing such a thing if general health is poor. Take the health of this ministry for example! Columns haven't been filled in, civil servants aren't here. Bureaucracy. And what do you think about such disgusting inflation?!"

"Intolerable...." I replied, following him with considerable difficulty.

"The world's in poor health too," he continued. "Hitler is a vile tumor, and the Allies are yet another. And what about the religious endowments you have here? Why should some rabble be entitled to thousands and thousands of pounds?!"

My head was spinning but I managed to reply. "Let's hope that things will turn out well," I said, " as long as our Pasha – the Prime Minister – is concerned about problems like these!"

He stood up suddenly! "But when will the Minister be here?" he asked. "Ten o'clock! And what about the Director of the office? Nine o'clock...."

He looked at the time and then sat down looking gloomy. He glanced at the calendar on the wall; Wednesday the 2nd of June, 29th of Jamadi al-Awwal, 25th of Bashans.*

"How many sheets of the calendar will go by," he asked in a bored tone, "before things are as sound as they should be?"

He stared at me provocatively. I was totally unnerved. But he soon changed his expression and looked jovial. "What do you want out of life?" he asked.

I felt baffled and preferred to remain silent. When I realized that he was waiting for my reply, I used my hand to make some obscure gesture which could say what I wanted before my tongue did. "Many things!" I replied.

"For example!"

I summoned up my courage. "A decent salary...."

"What about good health?..."

"That's not bad either...."

"How much money do you want?"

"Enough...."

"Enough for what?"

"For the necessities of life and important luxuries. I want to have a family...."

"Don't other people need that too?"

* Muslim and Coptic calendar months.

"Yes. Why not!?"

"And that's the way people can be saved from vile emotions, is it?"

"Yes, Sir...." I replied with genuine delight. "No!" he said scoffing angrily. "That's not enough."

"There's still Hitler and Churchill too. That's the baffling problem. I've been asked to look into it, but every time I find a solution, I find myself facing another problem. Every time I get rid of one sore, another one appears. It's as if the journey has to comprise the entire world...."

"The world!" I muttered in amazement.

"Yes, the world. If you need any proof, just look at the effects of the war on our country. Many complicated things, countless problems. Just imagine you want to enjoy yourself in the Swiss mountains and then you're told that the area is threatened by a German invasion; or that you're sitting under the shade of Buddha's tree in India and then find that the atmosphere is weighed down with fanaticism and explosions. Perhaps you want to visit Moscow, but you'll never return. And the overpricing? It's reached inconceivable levels, hasn't it?!"

My imagination was gasping for breath. I no longer understood a word, but clung tenaciously to the little bit in which I could detect some meaning.

"The prices are utterly disgusting. Tomatoes are very scarce, and potatoes have become a myth...."

You could tell through his dark glasses that he was thinking; he seemed a little sad and listless. "Would these problems be solved," he asked, "if we fixed salaries?"

"Which salaries, Sir?"

"A decree would be issued saying that the highest salaries could not be more than so much...."

"So much?"

"Wouldn't the tomatoes reappear as a result and potatoes as well? The rents of apartments and houses would come down too, wouldn't they?"

"But the world doesn't consist of just civil servants.

There are merchants, industrialists and land owners. And then there are foreigners as well!"

He shook his head as though he were tired. "There's Hitler, Mussolini and Churchill; countless lies and cries from the blacks to deafen your ears...."

What a strange person he was. He was not a tyrant like other counsellors, nor was he as terrifying as other top officials. He had a gentle side to him which could hardly be distinguished from...what shall I say...jesting! However, I decided to be very wary till the end. "These are bewildering things," I replied gently and hopefully. "The problems they pose cannot be solved, or, if they can, it will take a long time, longer than anyone can conceive. But isn't there an easy way to do it, if only you can convince the Minister for example to raise the subsidies?!"

He looked at me in amazement. "Do you want me to change my important assignment into a personal effort to make things better for you?" he asked.

I felt my face burning with shame. "I didn't mean that; I just...." I stammered.

He interrupted me forcefully. "What's wrong with us is that we're always thinking of ourselves and never about other people."

He looked at the time. "The Minister at ten, the Director of the office at nine," he said angrily. "The whole point of my arriving early is wasted!"

Just then, I remembered something I should have done long ago if it hadn't been for the fact that I was so flustered. "I didn't order you any coffee, Sir!" I shouted.

I stretched out my hands towards the bell, but he stopped me with an angry, imperious gesture. "We're in a cemetery, not a cafe!" he said angrily, and then continued in a gentle tone of voice. "I said what was wrong with us was that we think of ourselves and no one else," he said. "The truth is that I have the power to be happy in myself. All I have to do is to abandon the world and all its anxieties; that's real happiness where I can listen in its empty silence to the music of the stars. But I can't; I don't want to. Even worries have their own melodies to which the heart can tune in. Either general health or none at all; that's my final creed. That's why I was given the assignment!"

He started playing with the hair of his fly whisk. I felt bewildered. What did he mean, I asked myself! What was there behind those dark glasses? At that moment, the door opened and a messenger appeared.

"The Director has arrived," he said as usual.

I excused myself and went into the Director's office immediately. "Ismail Bey al-Bajuri, the Counsellor to the Prime Minister, is in my office," I told him.

The Director leapt to his feet. "Ismail Bey al-Bajuri?" he asked.

Next moment, he was shaking his hand respectfully and putting himself at his disposal. Then they both went into the Director's office and I was left on my own to think. I was still feeling overwhelmed by the meeting and the questions it had raised.

I carried on looking through the newspapers, feeling very distracted. I could not concentrate on anything I was doing. This went on for half an hour or thereabouts. Suddenly the door opened and the Director of the office rushed in. He made for the telephone. "Do you know this counsellor?" he asked me.

I replied that I did not.

He turned the bell on the telephone. "Hello, is that the Prime Minister's office? This is Ali Abbas, the Director of the Minister of Religious endowments office. Could you tell me, please; do you have someone called Ismail Bey al-Bajuri as a counsellor in your office.... You're sure about that, Sir! We've got someone here of that name and description; it's written on his card.... I'm sorry to have bothered you. I'll do what you suggest."

He put the receiver down without looking at my stunned expression. Then he turned the bell a second time. "Hello, is that the ma'mur?...this is Ali Abbas, Director of the Minister of Religious Endowments office. We've got someone here pretending to be from the Prime Minister's office. He's saying strange things and asking to meet the Minister himself. Bearing in mind the precarious situation the country is going through at the moment, I'm afraid he might be a terrorist...it's true that he doesn't look like the usual type of young man, but I'm worried about the surprise element.... I'll be waiting for you, Sir. Please hurry...."

He put down the receiver and left the room immediately with me following. The whole thing was explained at the station. He was not a terrorist, he was just crazy. His family was called and the usual measures were taken.

I heard him speak to the *ma'mur* in a tone of vexed arrogance. "It's all my fault," he said. "It wasn't easier to enjoy peace of mind. It's my fault...."

The Whisper of Madness

What is madness?

It seems to be a condition as inscrutable as life and death. You can learn a great deal about it when you look at it from the outside, but its substance and real essence remain a closed secret. Our friend knows now that he stayed for a while as a guest in Khanka*. Like all sane people, he can still remember his past life and is fully aware of his present one as well. But, when it comes to remembering about that short period – it was short, thank God – he is completely at a loss and cannot be certain of anything. It was a journey into a marvellous ethereal world filled with mist. Faces from this world floating front of his eyes, but he cannot make out their features. Every time he tries to use his memory to throw some light on them, they fly away and are swallowed up in darkness. Sometimes he hears something which sounds like a whisper, and, if he really concentrates, he can make out the various places where he hears them; until, that is, they run away and leave behind a sense of silence and bewilderment.

That magical period is now lost forever and the pleasures and pain which went with it. Even the people who were alive during that remarkable period have drawn a thick veil of silence and pretended ignorance over it for some undeclared reason. So it has fallen into oblivion without any reliable historian being allowed to record its wonders. How did it happen, I ask myself? When did it happen? How did people realize that someone had lost his reason,

* Khanka: a mental asylum in Cairo.

45

and that this person had become an eccentric who had to be kept away from people, like some wild beast?!

He was a quiet man, and this absolute quietness was his own special characteristic. Perhaps that was why he liked to be apathetic and lazy, withdrew from contact with other people and refused to exert himself in any way. That was why he left school at an early age and refused to do any work; he was happy with another fairly good source of income. The thing he liked best was to sit quietly in an isolated seat in the pavement cafe, interlock his hands over his knee, and spend hour after hour sitting there without moving or saying a word. He would sit there with a sleepy look and drooping eyelids, watching the people coming and going. He never got bored, tired or worried; his whole life involved sitting on this particular chair on the pavement and it gave him the greatest pleasure. However, behind this silent and stupid exterior, there was nothing; no warmth or movement deep down inside him or even in his imagination. His quietness was complete, inside and out, mind and body, feelings and imagination. He was a statue of flesh and blood, seeming to watch people as they passed by, but really isolated from life.

Then what?!

In this stagnant, brackish water, there was a sudden strange movement as though someone had thrown a stone into it.

How?!

One day, he was sitting quietly on his seat on the pavement and noticed some workers filling up the whole street in advance of a spectacular parade. They were sprinkling bright yellow sand, much to the delight of the people who were watching. For the first time in his life, something astonished him. Why were they sprinkling sand, he asked himself. It would get blown about and would fill people's nostrils and hurt them. The same people would soon come back, brush it all up and collect it again. So why sprinkle it at all?! Perhaps the whole thing was too paltry to demand questions or justify any feeling of bewilderment. But to him, the question seemed to be the most important truth in his life at that moment. He imagined that he was dealing with one of the greatest problems of the universe: In all this sprinking followed by sweeping up, with people being hurt in between the two operations, he found a bewildering problem. He even felt like laughing, which was something he rarely did; but this time he laughed and laughed till his eyes were running. This laughter was no mere sudden emotion; in fact, it was the sign of a complete change which brought him out of his terrible silence to a totally new attitude. He spent his day either in a state of bewilderment or else laughing. He kept on talking to himself in a sort of a daze: — "They sprinkle, then they hurt people, then they sweep...Ha, Ha, Ha!"

Next morning, he had not recovered from his bewilderment. He stood in front of the mirror getting ready to go out. His eyes fell on his tie and he soon felt baffled all over again. Why, he asked himself, did he tie his tie like that? What was the point of a tie? Why do we put ourselves to the trouble of having to choose a color and material? Before he realized it, he was laughing again as he had done the day before. He started looking at the tie in helpless confusion. He looked at the various parts of his outfit with a feeling of rejection and alienation. What was the point, he asked himself, of hiding ourselves in this laughable fashion? Why did we not take these clothes off and throw them on the ground? Why did we not appear as God created us? However, he continued to put his clothes on until he was fully dressed, and then went out of the house as usual.

He no longer felt that compact quietness which had lived peacefully beneath his skin for so long. How could he relax when these heavy clothes were beginning to strangle him in spite of himself?! Yes, in spite of himself. A wave of anger came over him as he hurried along. It annoyed him to have to accept any restrictions in spite of himself. Wasn't mankind free? He thought for a moment and then replied enthusiastically, "Yes, I'm free." Suddenly he felt filled with the spirit of freedom; its light illuminated every part of his soul until he felt overjoyed. Yes, he was free. Freedom came to him like a revelation. He was quite certain about it, and there was no room for doubt. He was free to do what he wished, how he wished, when he wished, without submitting to any force or giving way to any factors internal or external. The problem of free-will was solved in one second, and, with incredible enthusiasm, he rescued it from the heavy tread of pretexts. He had a remarkable feeling of happiness and superiority. He looked disdainfully at people as they strolled along the sides of the road in fetters, powerless to control their own fate, be it good or bad. When they walked, they could not stop; when they stopped, they could not walk. He, on the other hand, could walk when he wished and stop when he wished; even more, he could despise every force, every law, every instinct. This exciting new feeling encouraged him to test out his extraordinary power; he could not resist the call of freedom.

He stopped suddenly as he was walking. "Here I am," he told himself. "I've stopped for no reason at all." He looked around him for a few seconds, and then asked himself whether he could lift his hands up without bothering about anyone else. Then he asked himself again whether he could find the courage to stand on one leg. "Why shouldn't I?" he asked himself, "What is there to hamper my freedom?" he started lifting his left leg as though he were doing a gymnastic exercise; he was concentrating hard and not worrying about anything else as though he were the only person on the road and no one were watching him. A sense of serenity and contentment filled his heart, and he had a feeling of boundless self-confidence. He began to regret the opportunities he had missed all his life when he could have enjoyed his freedom and happiness. He carried on walking as though he were facing life all over again.

On his way to the cafe, he passed by a restaurant where he would sometimes eat his dinner. He noticed a table on the pavement filled with delicious things. A man and woman were sitting at it facing each other; they were both eating and drinking with gusto. A short distance away, a group of street urchins was crouching. They were completely naked except for a few torn rags, and their faces and skin were covered with a thick layer of dust and filth. The disparity between the two groups of people displeased him, and his sense of freedom shared in his displeasure and refused to allow him to walk past the restaurant in haughty disdain. But what could he do? The urchins must eat along with those other people, his heart told him with confidence and conviction. But the others will not give up any of the delicious chicken they have in front of them without a fight, that is certain! If he threw it on the ground, it would get covered in dust. There was no power which could deprive the urchins of having it; so was there anything to stop him carrying out his wish?...Go on! Dithering may have been feasible in the old days, but now ...Quietly, he went up to the table, stretched out his hand to the tray and took the chicken. He then threw it at the feet of the naked children, turned away from the table and proceeded on his way as though he had done nothing wrong. He paid no attention to the yelling and screaming full of the most obscene oaths and curses which pursued him. In fact, he could not help laughing and started doing so uncontrollably till his eyes began to run. He sighed with satisfaction from deep down inside him, and his confidence and happiness and a profound sense of calm came back to him.

He reached the cafe and proceeded to his chair as usual, but this time, he could not interlock his hands over his knees and then abandon himself to his usual silence. His own self would not obey him. He had lost his power to sit still, or else had been cured of the inability to move. You could see it from the way he was sitting there. He was on the point of getting up then, at that very moment, he saw someone who was no stranger to him although they had not been formally introduced. Like him, this man was one of the cafe regulars. He was portly and swaggered along with his head held high in disdain. He looked at the people round him with an arrogant contempt, and every movement he made spoke of vanity and pride. It seemed as though humanity aroused in him the feelings which worms* can arouse in the minds of sensitive people.. It was as though he were seeing this man for the first time; his ugliness and eccentricity were exposed. The strange laughter which had kept on teasing him for these two days got the better of him. He did not take his eyes off this man and focused in particular on his neck which protruded from the gusset of his shirt, broad, full and enticing. He asked himself whether he could let him pass by in peace?? God forbid! He had met the missionary of freedom and had promised not to let him down in any way. He shrugged his shoulders indifferently and came up to the man till he was almost touching him. He lifted his hand and brought it down on the nape of the man's neck with all the force he could muster. The thump of the blow echoed around. He could not control himself and burst into laughter. However, this experiment did not end quite as innocuously as the previous one. The man turned round and faced towards him with an insane anger written all over his face. He grabbed hold of his collar and pummelled and kicked him till some of the people sitting around pulled them apart. He left the cafe panting. Remarkably enough, he did not feel annoyed or sorry; on the contrary, he felt a strange pleasure which he had never experienced before. His mouth displayed a lingering smile. His heart was overflowing with a vitality and joy which overcame any feeling of pain. He no longer cared about anything except the freedom which he had won in a happy moment of time. He refused to relinquish it for a single second of his life. From then on, he threw himself into an ever-increasing stream of risky experiments with an unbendable will and uncontrollable force. He cuffed

* Worms having connections with the dead in their graves.

people's necks, spat in their faces and kicked them front and back. He did not escape without being punched or cursed on every occasion. His glasses were smashed, the tassel on his *tarbush** was torn, his shirt was ripped and his trousers were spoiled. But he could not be stopped, restrained or turned from his course, fraught with dangers though it was. The smile never left his lips, and the drunkenness which was affecting his besotted heart did not abate. If death itself had blocked his path, he would have plunged into the attack without fear.

Just as the sun was on the point of setting, his wandering eyes noticed a beautiful girl coming towards him with her arm in that of an elegant-looking man. She was strutting along in a thin, transparent dress, and the nipples of her breasts were almost breaking through the material of her silk gown. Her ample bosom caught his eyes and they grew wider as his astonishment increased. The view staggered him. She came closer and closer till she was at arm's length. His mind – or his madness – was thinking at an imaginary speed. He imagined that he was touching those wayward breasts – some man would be doing it in any case...so let it be this man. He stood in her way, stretched out his hand with lightning speed and pinched her. Oh dear! What a hail of blows and punches fell on him! Many people joined in but eventually they left him alone! Maybe it was his insane laughter which made them afraid, or perhaps the look in his staring eyes alarmed them. In any case, they left him. So he escaped and was hardly the worse for wear! He was still eager for more adventure. But he took a look at his clothes, and was shocked to find them so torn and ripped. However, instead of feeling sorry for himself, he began to remember what he had been thinking about the day before when he was standing in front of the mirror. A strange look appeared in his eyes, and he started asking himself again why he

* Fez

allowed himself to remain a prisoner in these stupid wrappings which constricted his chest, stomach and legs?! He felt weighed down by them, as though the pressure which they exerted was strangling him. He exploded; he could not stand them any longer. His hands started to tear them off one by one without the slightest pause for thought. He had stripped himself of all his clothes, and stood there as naked as God created him. His strange laughter toyed with him and he guffawed. Then he dashed off on his way....

Child's Paradise

"Daddy."

"Yes."

"My friend Nadia and I are always together...."

"Of course, darling; she's your friend."

"In class, on walks, at meal times...."

"That's marvellous. She is a pretty girl with good manners."

"But when the religion lesson comes, I go into one room, and she goes into another. Why is that?"

He looked at her mother and saw that she was smiling though she was busy embroidering.

"That's only for the religion lesson...." he replied with a smile.

"Why, Daddy?"

"Because you belong to one religion, and she belongs to another."

"How is that, Daddy?"

"You are a Muslim and she is Christian."

"Why, Daddy?"

"You're very young. You will learn later on."

"I'm a big girl, Daddy."

"No, you're not; you're a little girl, my darling."

"Why am I a Muslim?"

He had to be patient and cautious; he shouldn't give up the principles of modern education at first attempt.

"Daddy is a Muslim and Mummy is a Muslim," he replied, "and so you're a Muslim too."

"And Nadia?"

"Her father's a Christian and her mother is too, and so

she is a Christian."

"Is it because her father wears glasses?"

"No, no. It's got nothing to do with wearing glasses. It's because her grandfather was a Christian as well...."

He decided to continue the chain of ancestors all the way to infinity so that she would get bored and change the subject. But instead she asked, "Which is better?"

He thought for a moment. "Being a Muslim girl is good," he said, "and so is being a Christian girl...."

"Mustn't one be better than the other?"

"One is good and so is the other."

"Shall I be made into a Christian so that we can always be together?"

"No, no, darling; that's impossible. Every little girl stays just like her Daddy and Mummy...."

"But why?"

This modern education was really tough! "Won't you wait till you grow up?" he asked her.

"No, Daddy...."

"All right. You know all about fashion; some people like one style and others prefer another. Your being a Muslim is the latest fashion, and so you must stay a Muslim...."

"You mean, Nadia is old-fashioned?"

Blast you and Nadia, both of you! It was obvious that, in spite of all the care he had taken, he had made a mistake and was being driven mercilessly into a bottle neck. "It's a question of taste," he replied "But every little girl must stay like her Daddy and Mummy...."

"Shall I tell her that she's old-fashioned and that I'm up-to-date?"

"Every religion is good," he replied quickly. "Muslim girls worship God, and so do Christians...."

"Why does she worship Him in one room and I in another?"

"In one room, they worship Him in one way, and in the other room, in another way...."

"What's the difference, Daddy?"

"You will learn about it in the coming year or else the year after that. For the moment, it's enough for you to know that a Muslim little girl worships God and a Christian little girl does too."

"Who is God, Daddy?"

He had been caught. He thought for a while. "What did teacher say at school?" he asked to get a bit of leeway.

"She reads the chapter from the Qur'an and teaches us the prayers, but I don't know. Who is God, Daddy?"

He thought for a while. "He is the Creator of the whole world," he replied with an enigmatic smile.

"All of it?"

"All of it."

"What does Creator mean, Daddy?"

"It means that he makes everything."

"How, Daddy?"

"With a mighty power."

"Where does he live?"

"In the whole world."

"What about the time before the world?"

"He lived up there...."

"In Heaven?"

"Yes."

"I want to see Him."

"Impossible."

"Not even on television?"

"That's impossible too."

"Can't anyone see Him?"

"No."

"How do you know that He's up there?"

"That's the way He is."

"Who knows He's up there?"

"The prophets."

"The prophets?"

"Yes, like our lord Muhammad."

"How, Daddy?"

"Through a special power he had."

"Has he got powerful eyes?"

"Yes."

"Why. Daddy?"

"That's how God created him."

"Why, Daddy?"

"He is free to do what He wishes," he replied, controlling his flagging patience.

"And how does he see Him?"

"Very mighty, very powerful, capable of doing anything."

"Like you, Daddy?"

"There is no one like Him," he replied, suppressing a laugh.

"Why does He live up there?"

"The earth is not big enough for Him, but He sees everything."

For a moment she was distracted. "But Nadia told me that He lived on the earth," she said.

"Because He sees everywhere, it seems as if He is living everywhere."

"She said that people killed Him!?"

"But He is alive, He doesn't die."

"Nadia said they killed Him...."

"No, no, my darling. They thought they killed Him, but He's alive, He doesn't die."

"Is my grandfather alive too?"

"No, he is dead."

"Did people kill him?"

"No, he died of his own accord...."

"How?"

"He was ill, then he died...."

"Will my sister die because she is ill?" He frowned a little, noticing a gesture of protest coming from her mother's direction.

"No, no, she will get better, God willing."

"Why did my grandfather die?"

"He was an old man when he fell ill...."

"You fell ill and you're old. Why didn't you die?" Her mother scolded her. The little girl looked at the two of them in bewilderment.

"We all die when God wishes it," her father replied.

"Why does God want us to die?"

"He is free to do what He wishes."

"Is death nice?"

"No, my sweet...."

"Why does God want something which isn't nice?"

"It is nice as long as God wants it for us."

"But you said it wasn't nice."

"I was wrong, darling...."

"Why was Mummy angry when I said you would die?"

"Because God doesn't want that yet."

"Why does He want it, Daddy?"

"He brings us here, and then takes us away."

"Why, Daddy?"

"So that we can do nice things here before we leave."

"Why don't we stay?"

"The world wouldn't be large enough for everyone if they all stayed."

"And do we leave the nice things behind?"

"We will be going on to much nicer things than them."

"Where?"

"Up there."

"Where God is?"

"Yes."

"Will we see Him?"

"Yes."

"Is that nice?"

"Of course."

"Do we have to go then?"

"We haven't done any nice things yet."

"Did my grandfather do some nice things?"

"Yes...."

"What did he do?"

"He built a house and grew plants in a garden..."

"What did my cousin Toto do?"

He frowned for a moment, then glanced sympathetically at her mother. "He built a little house too before he went...." he continued.

"But our neighbor Lu'lu hits me and never does anything nice."

"He's a naughty boy."

"But he will never die!"

"Only when God wishes it...."

"Even though he never does anything nice?"

"Everyone dies. Those who do good things go to God, and those who do bad things go to Hell...."

She sighed and then was silent. He was well aware of how much pressure he was under, and didn't know how much of what he had said was right and how much was wrong. The stream of questions had aroused question marks deep down inside him.

"I want to stay with Nadia all the time," the little girl shouted after a little while.

He looked at her in curiosity.

"Even in the religion lesson!" she continued. He laughed loudly, and so did her mother. "I don't think it's possible to discuss these questions on that level!" he said with a yawn.

"One day she will grow up," his wife said, "and then you'll be able to offer her all these facts you seem to know!!!"

He turned angrily in her direction to see whether she really meant what she said, or was just being sarcastic. He found her engrossed once again in her embroidery.

Shahrazad

"Hello!"

"Professor Mahmud Shukri?"

"Yes. Who's speaking?"

"Excuse me for bothering you without being introduced."

"That's quite all right. To whom am I speaking?"

"The name's not important, but I'm one of the thousands of women who pose you their problems...."

"I'm at your service, Miss."

"Mrs., please."

"I'm at your service then, Madam."

"It's a long story."

"Perhaps it would be better if you wrote to me."

"I'm no good at writing."

"Could you come and see me in the magazine office?"

"I haven't got the nerve; at least, not now!"

He paused for a few moments at the word 'now'! He smiled as he savoured her soft voice. "What then?" he asked.

"I'd like you to allow me to take up a few minutes of your time every day or else whenever your busy schedule allows you some time...."

"That's funny; it reminds me of Shahrazad!"

"Shahrazad! That's an attractive name. Allow me to borrow it temporarily."

He laughed. "And this is Shahrayar listening to you!" he said.

She laughed too. He found her laughter as delightful as her voice.

"Don't expect me to present you with a neat and well-defined problem," she continued. "It's a long story as I told you, and it's a miserable one as well...."

"I only hope I can live up to your good opinion of me."

"Please stop me any way you like if I take up more time than you have allowed for me...."

"As you say."

"I've taken up a good deal of your time today already so let's postpone the story till tomorrow. For the moment, it's sufficient for me to confess that I felt drawn towards you by the humane spirit of your writings."

"Thank you."

"And not just by your writings either, but by your photograph as well!"

"My photograph?" he asked pursuing the subject with interest.

"Yes, I read in your big eyes a look of intelligence and humane sympathy which seem to issue an invitation to anyone who was looking for consolation...."

"Thanks again," he said, and then continued with a laugh, "you're saying such kind things, it's like a love-poem."

"It's an expression of hope that there is – still – some hope left in the world."

He put down the receiver, smiled, and then frowned for a moment as he thought. Then he smiled again.

2

"Hello!"

"Shahrazad here!"

"How are you? I've been waiting for you."

"I'll get straight on with the subject so as not to waste your time."

"I'm listening...."

"I grew up as an orphan without a mother. Our father – I mean, the father of my sister and myself (she's two years younger than I) – remarried. We spent our adolesence without any love or affection. We only had a little education, and when our father died, we moved to our uncle's house. Each of us had an allowance of about five pounds."

"This is all ancient history, isn't it?

"To a certain extent, yes, but it's all necessary. We weren't happy in our uncle's house; he regarded us as a real burden and we felt lonely and miserable. We used to give him every millieme of our allowance and started to work in the house without any objections. The problem was simply one of bad luck; no more, no less...."

"I understand. What a shame.!"

"Then an officer came to ask for my hand. We had inherited an old house from our father, and my uncle sold it. With my share he bought me an inexpensive trousseau. My husband understood from the very beginning what our situation really was, but he did not change his mind. The truth was that we lived a real love story life, as they say. This continued even after we were married...."

"I wonder whether the way you're talking about this love story doesn't betray a certain reserve?"

"Never mind. The terrible thing was that he was extravagant. He spent everything he had like an idiot and without any thought of what the consequences would be. I didn't know how to cure him of it; I tried and tried, but without success...."

"On this point,.....I mean,... aren't you partly to blame?"

"No, no, believe me. All I wanted was to live a happy life. I wanted it because my love was so fervent and I'd suffered such misery and contempt before...."

"That's understandable!"

"It sounds as if you don't believe me. I can still remember what you said about a wife's responsibility for her own husband's misbehaviour. But what else could I do? I begged him gently, I threatened, I pleaded; I asked him to give me the money I needed to run the house at the beginning of the month. His usual reply was to bring me home a group of his friends, and then all night it would be "Bring some food, bring drink." This would go on till dawn. The night would be spent on festivities, but we would feel the pinch the next morning!"

"What happened on other days?"

"He'd ask me to go to my uncle for help, but that was impossible; or else to borrow from my sister, and that was impossible too since she was about to get married. Meanwhile, he kept borrowing money from his family. Our whole life became a despicable sham, something very regrettable."

"That's true...."

"The marriage broke up and came to its predestined end, namely divorce. After losing my allowance, I moved to my sister's house and had to put up with a bitter and humiliating existence...."

"Could that be the problem?"

"Wait a moment. We're still in the past. But I won't take up much more of your time. After a year, my husband – from whom I had been divorced – asked me to take him back again. He told me that he wanted us to start our married life again and assured me that life had taught him a lesson. He took me to a pension in Qasr an-Nil Street where he was living so that we could plan our future life. As soon as the door of his room was closed, he hugged me and repeated that since he'd left me, he'd got no enjoyment out of life."

"And you gave in to him."

"I didn't feel I was dealing with a strange man. For most of the time, we began discussing the steps involved in our getting married again. As we parted he promised to go and see my uncle the very next morning."

"Your voice has got lower and changed, hasn't it?"

"Yes. I found out afterwards that, when he asked me to meet him again, he was already engaged for the second time and he was married a week later. The whole thing had just been a whim which he wanted to get out of his system

before beginning his new life...."
"The miserable wretch...."
"Yes. I won't bother you any more. Till next time...."

3

"Hello!"
"Sharazad here!"
"Hello!"
"Am I disturbing you?"
"On the contrary, please carry on."
"Well, I stayed with my sister for a while, but as time went by, I began to feel that it wasn't really desirable!"
"Why?"
"That was just the way I felt. I wasn't wrong either...."
"How could that be when she's your sister and suffered through the same terrible childhood you did?"
"The inevitable happened!"
"Her husband?"
"Close!"
"He didn't like having you in his house?"
"Almost it. The important thing is that I was forced to leave so as to keep my relationship with my sister intact...."
"You didn't mention the reason explicitly. Allow me to quess. Was it jealousy perhaps?!"
"Imaginary jealousy is more like it!"
"Did you go to your uncle's house?"
"He'd died. I rented a small apartment...."
"How did you get the money?"
I sold as much of my trousseau as I could and started to look for a job...any job. It was terribly fruitless; continuous searching and hunger. Believe me, I've known terrible hunger; the whole day would go by without any food to eat, or rather any food worth mentioning. I found myself tempted once to accept one of the suggestions which would be aimed in my direction on the street, but I put off giving in to them in the hope that God's mercy would catch up with

me before I finally fell. I used to look out of my window in the tranquil night and gaze up at the sky. "Merciful God," I would shout deep down inside me, "I'm hungry, I'm dying of hunger." Every time my strength started to give out, I would visit my sister to have a wholesome meal, but no one asked how I was because they were afraid that the answer I gave would imply a responsibility which they preferred to ignore!"

"Unbelievably callous...."

"One day, I read an advertisement in the paper asking for a housekeeper for an old man in return for board and lodging, as well as salary."

"Manna from Heaven."

"I rushed over without delay and rented out my apartment...."

"A merciful conclusion, especially if the old man just needed looking after and nothing else!"

"He was very old. I served him loyally; I was very good at housework in every sense of the word. I was cook, waitress, nurse, all at once, and even read the newspaper to him...."

"Fine, fine..."

"Now I was well fed after being hungry for such a long time. After I'd felt so afraid, I now felt secure and prayed to God that the old man might live forever...."

"Then what happened, I wonder?"

"One day, I was reading the paper to him when my eyes fell on an advertisement asking for a housekeeper for an old man; the reader was directed to our house!!"

"Oh, no!"

"Yes. I was aghast. I read it to him, but he turned away without denying it. I asked him why he wanted to dispense with my services and why he was tired of me, but he didn't open his mouth...."

"Very peculiar. There must have been a reason."

"Absolutely nothing on my part at all!"

"Was there anything between the two of you apart from

house-keeping?"

"Almost nothing!"

"What's that supposed to mean?! Please be frank."

"Sometimes, he would ask me to stand in front of him naked!"

"And you refused?"

"No. I did as he asked...."

"Then why was he looking for someone else?"

"How should I know? He said he wanted innovations. Whatever he thought, I begged him to change his mind. I told him I was alone and poor and that he was the only person I had in the world. But he persisted in dismissing me and said nothing more. I felt he was as hateful as death and so I saw no alternative but to leave...."

4

"Hello!"

"Sharazad here, Professor! How are you?"

"Hallo! Sharazad, your story is keeping me completely absorbed."

"Thank you, Professor. My heart certainly didn't deceive me when it told me to get in touch with you. Now let's carry on with the story. I returned home and told the tenant – he was a simple civil servant of forty – that I needed my apartment again. He refused to consider vacating it however, and, when he learned of my predicament, he suggested that I stay there with him! I didn't think twice before accepting. In fact, my will had broken down and nothing mattered...."

"Did you think his invitation meant?...."

"He put me in one of the two rooms which made up the apartment. After that, everthing was clearly understood!"

"From the very first night?!"

"Yes. He was really a nice friendly man...."

"Incredible...."

"Wait a minute. It was for that reason that I lost him!"

"What a tale this is!"

"One day, he told me I was getting attached to him and vice versa, and so we would have to separate!"

"Separate!"

"Yes, separate...I expected him to say get married, but instead he said 'separate'."

"Unbelievable!"

"I asked him what he meant. He replied in a trenchant tone of voice that there were things to stop him getting mar-ried and so we would have to separate. I told him pleadingly that I didn't ask him to marry me and had no intention of doing so, so why couldn't we stay as we were. He replied that it was a strange life and that one day I would find myself alone in my old age with no means of support and no rights. There was nothing for it but to separate, he said...."

"What a strange man! He sounds fine on the surface, but he's either selfish or clever..."

"The important thing is that he left, and I found myself alone yet again and threatened with hunger..."

"What a shame!"

"I went through some bitter experiences. You under-stand, of course. But then I heard about a new law govern-ing allowance which permitted divorcees to get back their allowance for the first time. It clearly applied to me..."

"Thank heavens!"

"It wasn't enough of course, but I was used to a hard life. I'd learned how to sew and earned a little money from that. Together with the allowance, it saved me from death through hunger or slinking down to the level of the streets..."

"At least, we've got to safe territory...."

"Thank God! But now we've also got to the real problem?!"

"The real problem?!"

"It can be summarised in one word: loneliness...."

"Loneliness!"

"No husband, no son, no friends, no lover. I spend day and night cooped up in a tiny apartment, deprived of any kind of entertainment. Whole months go by without my exchanging a word with a soul. I'm forever gloomy, muttering and frowning. Sometimes, I'm afraid that I'm losing my mind and that I may commit suicide..."

"No, no! You've stood up to worse that this courageously. One day, God will provide you with a decent husband...."

"Don't talk to me about a decent husband. A widower with two children asked me to marry him, but I refused without any hesitation. I don't trust anyone any more. If I'm divorced again, I'll lose my allowance. And that's my real capital..."

"But a man with two children obviously wants a wife because he needs her badly..."

"I hate the very idea of marriage. In my mind, it's associated with treason and hunger...."

"Reconsider...."

"Impossible. Anything but marriage. I haven't got the courage to repeat the same experiments again..."

"Then how can you get rid of your loneliness?"

"That's the problem!"

"But you're rejecting a favorable solution!"

"Anything but marriage!"

He thought for a moment. "What do you think of the idea of our getting together?" he asked.

"That would be a great honor!"

He smiled. A thought went through his mind as he was smiling. In all simplicity, she was asking him to be her friend and yet at the same time assuring him that she would never ask him to marry here. He was no fool! He needed some fresh adventure too, so why not? The important thing was for her to be as beautiful as her voice. But what was her story? Maybe it was true. Nothing was impossible. But then maybe it was false from the beginning to end, or else in certain appended details. The cinema had up the creative faculties in women. Maybe this... maybe that... But the important thing was that she should be as beautiful as her voice. On that basis, he would give her a new experience to add to her previous ones. It would have its sweet moments but would end bitterly like everything else in the world. He began to smile as he strummed on the top of his desk.

◆ ◆ ◆ ◆

Shahrazad came.

He looked her over carefully as he welcomed her, and then invited her to sit down. She was in her thirties and was not bad looking. There was something about her appearance which gave the impression of bitterness. Her smiling expression seemed almost blasé and painfully sad; but in general, she was not bad. In fact, she was really quite acceptable. It was certainly not out of the question that her story was true, and maybe she had not been lying except in what she had said about marriage. She could not possibly hate it, but had to say she did in order to hang on to the friendship she wished for with such genuine longing.

But what did all this have to do with him? This woman did not suit him at all, as a body or a personality. The poor girl had no idea about the glowing opportunities open to him. So he had to conceal his thwarted hopes and treat her seriously.

"Welcome," he said. "Your story really affected me deeply...."

"I'm very obliged to you, Professor," she said with a sigh.

"But you must face up to your life with your usual courage...."

"But I...."

He suddenly felt a desire to put an end to the meeting as soon as possible.

"Listen to me," he said interrupting. "you're a great

woman. Suffering sometimes makes us into great people. You're great even during your fleeting errors. You're great in your loneliness, and your greatness will be even more fulfilled when you put an end to your solitude through some stupendous act of courage. Madam, life only has any value, meaning or pupose when we believe in people, whatever harm they may do us; and in God Almighty, something which cannot be shaken whatever Destiny does and whatever course it takes!"

He looked into her eyes and saw a look swimming with tears and disappointment. She was clever too, cleverer that he'd thought. There she was, smiling slightly, but it embarrassed him a little. "I believe in God, Professor," she muttered.

He gestured angrily with his hand. "All is vanity apart from the Almighty..." he said.

The Drug Addict and the Bomb

The road did not look the same. The world seemed different. People were hurrying along in a fervor. The sidewalk was crowded, and the street was boiling over with a non-stop movement. Soldiers looked around at the scene from beneath their helmets with satanic glances. What was going on? Every time he tried to focus his memory, it flew away like dust in a hurricane. The only thing he could re-member was that he was on his way to the shop of his friend, Muhsin the presser. Muhsin, old chap, where are you?.... The road went on forever as though it were going to the moon. He was sagging, and his feet were almost giving way beneath him. The sun was shining with darkened rays. He managed a smile even though he felt so bewildered, and let out a laugh. He looked at people in curiosity; what was it that was making them hurry like this?! He wondered if he had his *tarbush** on; he could feel a quiver inside his head, but did not feel sure about his *tarbush*. He could not muster the energy or the will to raise his hand to make sure it was there, but he came across an antique furniture shop and headed towards it. He looked in a mirror which was leaning in the doorway, and saw that his *tarbush* was tilted backwards and showed the front part of his black hair. While he was looking at himself, he adjusted his tie. He felt his eyes looked puffed up and almost closed. In the road, the movement became even more intense and the din got louder. What was happening? He opened his mouth to hum a song, but soon forgot the words, which made him annoyed.

* Fez

However, a movement like quicksilver danced around inside him, and he began to feel happy and to smile. With the power he had at his disposal, he told himself, he could fly, plunge into the earth or speak to the people who lived at the pole. Here at last was the shop of Muhsin the presser. He completely forgot about the questions he had been posing himself on the way and his own bewilderment. When he came up to 'Uncle' Muhsin, he bowed in greeting as though he were in the presence of a king. He remained in this position for some time to show his gratitude and also out of sheer laziness. The presser smiled. "You shouldn't, Ayyub Efendi!....." he said, without stopping his work.

"You deserve even more than that....."

A boy put out a chair for him at the shop door. He straightened up again and repeated his greeting by raising his hand. Then he went over to the chair and sank into it. As he was looking at the presser, he pointed at his head. "It couldn't possibly have been better...." he said.

"Didn't I tell you so?" the presser replied proudly.

"Nothing like it!"

"I told you to take an ounce before it ran out, but you wouldn't believe me."

Sitting out there on the street made him think again of the questions he'd been asking himself and brought back his feeling of bewilderment. He asked what it was all about.

"You'll see the procession soon," the presser said.

"The procession?!"

"Wow!....the leader comes back from London, and now here are the soldiers spreading out for the witch hunt!"

Ayyub looked around unwittingly. The sun's rays were getting darker. The sreet was full of people.

"Why?" he asked.

The presser did not understand the point of his question. "It's a triumphant return," he said. "It'll lead to the fall of the present government...."

Ayyub looked up at the sky, and rested his head on the back of the chair without moving. The presser smiled.

"Aren't you happy the government's going to fall?" he asked.

Ayyub showed no signs of movement or concern. The presser stifled a laugh. "Tell me," he asked, "who's ruling the country now?"

He brought his head back to the normal position. It was as though he had not heard a thing.

"Aren't you happy the constitution's going to be restored?" his friend asked.

He started humming an obscure tune. The presser laughed. "The best of luck to you!!" he said.

Shouting could be heard in the distance. A spark of enthusiasm began to spread along the street, and the *ma'mur** yelled "To order" in a menacing tone of voice. The presser left his shop and started yelling along with the rest. Ayyub laughed without leaving his seat. The procession went past like an earthquake. and thousands and thousands of people followed in its wake. No one was left sitting on the street except for Ayyub, and he moved back against the wall to get out of the way of the people who were running past. He started singing softly; so softly that no one could hear him: 'If your luck runs out, your clever tricks won't help you any more.'

The *ma'mur* stood there in the middle of the road with his white uniform and red sash. The headlong flood of humanity steered clear of him, and passed by to his right and left. There were just a few isolated cases of antagonism from the soldiers, but then suddenly, a young man pounced on the *ma'mur* and aimed a vicious blow at his stomach. The *ma'mur* groaned and fell to the ground, while the young man fled like the wind. The tune stuck in Ayyub's throat. He stared at the scene and suppressed a temptation to snigger. He saw the soldiers start lunging at people at random with their clubs. Some detectives began to chase after the young man, but clashing waves of humanity prevented

* Chief

them from following him. Events were happening at a crazy speed. Guns were fired. Within seconds, people scattered down every alley till the whole street was empty, and shops were closed up. The *ma'mur* stood up again leaning on a lieutenant's arm. "It'll be too bad for you if you don't get him!..." he yelled at the chief detective.

All these goings on had tired Ayyub's eyes. He was the only person left there on the street; even the soldiers had chased after the people who were running away. He closed his eyes so as to relax a little, and was overcome by a fit of laughter as he sat there in the empty road. He looked round and saw that the presser's shop was closed. He tried to re-member the song but did not succeed. He closed his eyes again, but the sound of heavy footsteps made him open them again. He saw a detective coming towards him with a mean look on his face. How could the earth have ejected him like this? The detective came closer and closer till he blocked Ayyub's view of the street and the sky as well. Ayyub stared at him without saying a word; he felt terribly lonely.

"What's making you laugh, you rogue?" the detective asked him in a voice which cracked like a whip.

Ayyub cowered on his chair. "I wasn't laughing...." he muttered.

The detective put his face closer to Ayyub's. "You strike the *ma'mur* and then laugh, do you?" he yelled.

Ayyub stretched out his hands as though he were trying to protect himself from the detective's blows. "Heaven for-bid... I never left my seat...." he said.

"Do you think I'm blind, you serpent's son?"

He punched Ayyub hard and knocked him to the ground; his *tarbush* flew for twenty yards. Ayyub groaned without trying to get up, but the detective grabbed him by the tie until his face turned purple. Ayyub got up staggering. "This is all wrong...." he said in a broken voice, "I swear by God, I never left my seat all the time...."

"Shut up!...I didn't take my eyes off you for one moment...."

He cuffed Ayyub again, then took out his whistle and blew it. A force of soldiers came up, and the detective pointed at Ayyub. "Arrest the criminal who struck your *ma'mur*," he said.

A loud explosion echoed forth. Everyone froze in their tracks.

"That's a bomb...." one of the soldiers said. They all listened in silence, and then, once they had recovered from their amazement, they arrested Ayyub.

"I'm innocent," he shouted at the top of his voice, "I didn't hit anyone. I never left my seat...."

They took him to the police station and brought him into the *ma'mur's* office. The detective offered his greetings. "Here's the criminal, Sir," he said.

"That's wrong, I'm innocent..." Ayyub shouted.

"Where did you arrest him?" the *ma'mur* asked the detective as he stared viciously at Ayyub.

"I caught up with him at Abdin Palace Square. I kept on running after him without ever taking my eyes off him. He put up a fierce struggle, but I lay on top of him till the soldiers came to help me...."

The *ma'mur* continued to stare piercingly at him. "Hit me, would you, you son of a bitch!" he said in a fury.

"I swear to God...." Ayyub yelled out in despair. The *ma'mur* shut him up with a blow, and then gave the detective a special sign. "Don't leave any marks for the public attorney to see," he said.

The detective gave a bow to indicate that he understood, and then pushed Ayyub outside. He summoned his assistants, and they tied his hands behind his back. Then they started pummeling his face with their hands. He yelled out in agony and eventually fell to the ground in a faint. When he came round, he found himself laid out on a wooden bench surrounded by a cordon of soldiers. The detective dragged him up by the arm and he was taken to the *ma'mur's* office. This time, he was sat down in front of a group of officials in civilian clothes. His face felt so swollen that to him it almost filled up the whole room. Every part of his body and soul was in a state of collapse. The man whom he supposed to be their chief began to question him. "Are you ready to be questioned" he asked.

"I'm innocent!" he said in resignation.

He asked for something to drink, and they brought him a cup of water. The investigator asked him his name.

"Ayyub Hasan Tumara," he replied.

"What's your job....?"

"I'm a clerk at the Records Office."

"How old are you?"

"Thirty...."

"The soldiers and detectives saw you...."

"I'm innocent...." he interrupted, "by God's book, innocent...."

"Answer the questions and don't make a fuss...." the man said firmly.

"I didn't do anything...I don't know why I've been brought here...."

"The witnesses all say that you were the one who let off the bomb in front of tne Mixed Courts!"*

He did not understand a thing. They were either mad or drunk.

"I didn't leave my chair in front of the shop of Muhsin the presser," he replied, refusing to believe his own ears. "I didn't touch the *ma'mur....*"

"You're talking rubbish. It will only make things more difficult for you."

"I didn't do a thing...."

"You were the one who threw the bomb!"

"Bomb!.... Did you say bomb?!"

"Lots of soldiers and detectives saw you with their very own eyes."

* Mixed Courts: established in 1876 to hear cases involving foreigners in litigation with other foreigners and Egyptians.

"I don't understand a thing you're talking about" he said, hitting his forehead with his hand.

"What I'm saying is quite clear; just as clear as your foul crime.

"My dear Sir, I wasn't arrested on a charge of throwing a bomb. The detective arrested me without any reason, and then wrongly pinned the charge of assaulting the *ma'mur* on me."

"Confess; it'll help you. If you'll give us the names of the people who coerced you into committing the crime, you won't regret it...."

"Gentlemen, you're making a dreadful mistake," Ayyub yelled in a fractured voice. "I'm a poor man who has never assaulted anyone in his life. Ask Muhsin the presser...."

"Admit everything, you won't regret it."

"We know the people who are behind you," said a man sitting on the right of the investigator. "We'll read their names out to you and show you their photo that you can be quite sure we're telling the truth. You are indeed a poor devil, and they undoubtedly misled you. You were just a toy for them to play with in the most dastardly fashion. If you confess, that will make what you have done less serious, nothing at all in fact. But you must confess...."

"Confess!...but I didn't hit the *ma'mur*...."

"Where did you get the bomb?"

"Lord of heaven and earth...."

"So you're not prepared to confess!"

"Confess what?.... Don't you fear God?"

"Be warned. It's no use being stubborn."

He looked at the faces of the people who were staring at him, and saw a solid wall in front of him keeping all doors to pity and hope tight shut. A feeling of despair came over him in the midst of this terrible ordeal. "Do you really want me to confess?" he asked.

Their expressions changed and they began to show an interest which almost bordered on affection.

"Tell us, Ayyub," the investigator said.

"I confess that I'm a drug addict...."

Instead of interest, they seemed angry. "Are you kidding us?"

"There's half an ounce of it in my stomach. The court doctor can prove that for you...."

"You're destroying your future...."

"I'm high today as I am every day. Have you ever heard of a drug addict throwing a bomb?"

"That's just a childish trick to get out of it."

"I'm an alcoholic as well. I didn't strike the *ma'mur* or throw a bomb!"

"Careful, Ayyub...."

"Ask me why...I'll tell you. I've never bothered with politics all my life, I don't care whether you're talking about the 1930 or 1923 constitution. I've never yelled in a demonstration in my life. Bring the court doctor...."

"Follow my advice and confess. The names and photographs are in front of you...."

"Believe me, the only job I have in life is looking after ancient documents and sucking half an ounce a day. Bring the court doctor and ask anyone...."

A year went by before Ayyub returned to 'Uncle' Muhsin the presser's shop again. He was accused of throwing the bomb in the Mixed Courts; his picture was in the papers, and people looked at him as a self-sacrificing hero. A group of famous lawyers came forward to defend him, and the court found him innocent. The hall erupted into cheering. When he went back to the presser's shop, they embraced each other for a long time with great warmth. Then Ayyub took his usual seat in front of the shop.

"I've got some really good stuff!" Muhsin said in an affectionate greeting.

"I've spent a whole year without it," Ayyub replied with

a laugh, "and now I've forgotten about it...."

"Then it's about time you remembered...."

Ayyub didn't say a word.

"God send them all to Hell!" Muhsin said in amazement. "Ayyub Efendi, they've altered you so much, I hardly recognize you...."

Ayyub smiled without saying a word.

"But now people love and respect you!" Muhsin continued, feeling encouraged.

Ayyub gave an innocent, happy laugh.

"No one believes you're an addict," 'Uncle' Muhsin resumed, "but they do think you hit the *ma'mur* and threw the bomb...."

"The trial itself was like a bomb!" said Ayyub proudly.

"What do you plan to do now?" Muhsin asked doubtfully.

Ayyub thought for a while. "Some people have suggested that I put my name forward for the forthcoming elections!" he said.

Muhsin looked at him staggered. "But they know who threw the bomb!" he said.

"So what, even if they do?.... They said I refused to agree to have false charges trumped up against any of them...."

"But you don't care about anything on earth, do you?!"

"I married care and concern in the detention center and the court!" he replied with a smile.

The Singing Drunkard

There were no customers left in the tavern. The old waiter rubbed his bald head and yawned loudly like someone in pain. He started piling up the wooden chairs and bare tables. The owner walked all round the cramped premises, looking in every corner and in the lavatory. He counted up the *piastres* slowly, locked up the drawers underneath the table and the token drawer,* and then put out the lamp which was dangling over the table. The place became darker and looked much more gloomy.

"Hurry up," he told the waiter, "it's about two in the morning."

The waiter finished piling up the tables and chairs, and then took off his dirty apron which was stained in several places and hung it up on a nail in the wall. He walked towards the door, dragging his heavy feet which were buried inside a pair of rubber shoes. His skinny frame swayed around in an oversized *gallabiyya*. The owner put out the last light, and the place was plunged into darkness. He went outside, locked the door and left; his heavy shoes broke the silence in the street with their continuous squeaking noise.

Under the middle barrel inside the tavern a man was crouching. He watched impatiently as the two men left and listened to the sound of the squeaking shoes till it receded into the distance. Then, heaving a sigh of relief, he leapt out from under the barrel, and stood there, staring into the pitch darkness without being able to see a thing or even the

* In Egyptian cafes, tokens are often given in exchange for money before food and drink can be purchased.

semblance of anything. He was blind in every sense of the word, and felt utterly lost, as though he had been tossed into the world of the invisible. However, if the middle barrel was behind you, he told himself, then the bar must be to your left and the money box on the edge of the bar. He stretched out his arms in front of him, and made his way carefully to the left until his fingers touched the edge of the table. Resting his hand on it, he made his way along the side till he reached the high table. A strong smell of a mixture of pickled vegetables, sardines, and cheese filled his nostrils. He was completely lost, but...ah, here was the drawer he was looking for. Now he would find the money Manoli had made selling glasses of that wine of his which had been distilled in hellfire itself. He took an implement like a file out of his pocket and started applying it to the lock till it opened. Someone sneezed outside. His hand froze. He cursed and swore under his breath as he thought angrily of the person outside who would be groping along the narrow street in almost total darkness with only one lantern to light it at the end of the incline where it joined up with Al-Bawaki Street. He slid his hand impatiently into the drawer and felt around from one side to the other. He found nothing there, absolutely nothing. Manoli, the swine!! So, he thought, you take the takings away with you, do you? Don't you leave a single millieme behind? Isn't the money safer in the tavern than in the street or at home?

He frowned angrily, and the darkness made him feel even more annoyed. Was the whole venture to end in complete failure? Would the emptiness laugh at the ruse, the preparations, and the way everything had been worked out? He was so furious that he opened every drawer in the table, but all he found was some left-over Greek cheese, olives, and beans. He stood behind the table for a while in the cunning old man's place, thinking about nothing in particular and eating the bean seeds without enjoying them at all. Eventually, he had to admit it; he had lost. However, he decided to have a good time before using the window to escape. He stretched his hand out to the shelf behind him and took down a bottle of wine. He took the cork out, put his mouth over the top and started drinking greedily till he had emptied it. He concentrated hard so that he could follow the swirling eddy as it coursed through his stomach... awful...marvellous...priceless...nothing like it. There certainly was no better way of spending your money than on wine. There was no need to get angry. It was really a shame that you would have to miss taking the old women to the cemetery on your horse and cart tomorrow. God damn you, Manoli!! He stretched out his hand again and took another bottle. The darkness was really awful; he could not see a thing. Very well then, he told himself, he would go on drinking till his thirst was quenched, and postpone his decision to leave until the policeman did his rounds.

But the darkness was like a barrage; its breath smelled of wine and it had a rock-like grip. Here was a third bottle of the hell-water. You should sit down, he told himself so why not on top of the bar? Manoli had left and had taken the cash with him; so to Hell with Manoli!! Darkness is even more of a curse than Hell itself! He cleared his throat, and the sound reverberated around the tavern in the darkness. He was not particularly worried about it, nor was he really worried about worrying. The truth of the matter is, he told himself, you're an enemy of the dark. You work in the sunlight, sleep beneath the stars, and on winter nights the alley lantern lights up your basement bedroom. You've beaten up more men than you can count, you will throw yourself fearlessly at a stick, but you're afraid of tearing your only *gallabiyya*. Your donkey carries you along bareback, and yet no one worries that he is naked; but you cannot manage without clothes and drink. He lifted up the fourth bottle and you could hear the sound of him drinking as the wine trickled down his gullet; the noise reverberated around the walls in the dark silent room. Shaikh Zawi told me not to get drunk, he thought, but I told him I was Sultan of the Turks and Persians. "God damn you," he replied, whereupon I swore that I would call my donkey Az-Zawi.

He started humming softly: 'It's time for love, for love...'
He took down a fifth bottle, and then leaned on his palms
and stretched his legs out on the table. He remembered the
old scene of the poet with the *rebec* and asked himself why
lovely things disappear. He began to sing again as though he
were in his own home: 'It's time for love, for love – happiness is nigh.' The drunken melody came out all distorted
but he shook his head in admiration. As he sang the word
love, the orgasmic effect made him sing even louder. Then
he sat up and started clapping his hands.

Suddenly, there was a resounding knock on the door.

"Who's there?" yelled the policeman.

At first, he did not stop singing, but, when the knocking
continued, his gaiety deserted him and he stopped. "It's not
enough to do nothing worthwhile," he muttered to himself
angrily, 'But, damn it, to stop other people as well!"

"Who are you?" he asked arrogantly.

"I'm the policeman."

"What do you want?"

"Incredible!.... Tell me, who are you?"

"A customer!" he answered with a laugh.

"The whole world's asleep. How did you manage to stay
inside there?"

"What business is that of yours?"

"You drunken lecher, you'll pay for your cheek!"

"I haven't got a millieme on me!"

"Now I recognize your voice. Even though you're
drunk, I can still recognize it."

"Who doesn't know Ahmad Inaba.*

"The horse and cart man!"

"That's right...what can I do for you, Sergeant?"

The policeman blew his whistle and broke the nocturnal
silence. Inside the tavern, the man felt a wall above the

* Inaba means 'grape': perhaps Mahfuz also means to
imply 'easily squashed"?!

table till he came across the light switch and turned it on. He frowned and screwed up his eyes. Looking around the place carefully his bulging red eyes fell on the gas stove and its canister. His head was spinning and his thoughts with it; they were whirling around so fast that he could hardly hang on to anyone of them for even just a second. He almost forgot about the policeman's voice, but at that moment, he became aware of a big row going on outside. Oh dear! There was the station officer, the policeman, the cigarette-butt collectors who live on the pavements, and other people as well. He made out Manoli's voice.

"Manoli!" he yelled angrily.

"I'm Manoli, 'Uncle' Ahmad...." the man answered anxiously.

"Don't open the door...if I see any sign of the door moving at all your tavern will become one big sheet of flame...."

"No, no...don't burn yourself to death!"

"It's not me you're worried about, Manoli. There's gas everywhere; all around the floor, the barrels, the chairs and tables. I've got the match here in my hand....be careful, Manoli...."

"Calm down!" Manoli replied with obvious anxiety. "I won't open the door till you say so...."

"Where did you find such politeness all of a sudden, Manoli?"

"I've been polite all my life....calm down. Tell me what it is you want...."

"I've got everything I want."

"Don't you want to come out?" '

'No. And no one's to come in either."

"You can't stay in there forever!"

"That's quite possible. I've got everything I need here,"

"I'm sorry. I locked you in by mistake."

"You liar! And what's more, you know it!"

"But, really...that's what happened."

"You know very well that I'm here to steal."

"There's nothing in there worth stealing."

"What about the barrels of this poisonous wine?"

"Everything you've drunk is a present from me...."

"There isn't a millieme in the drawer...."

"I don't keep any money there...."

"Then why do you keep it locked, Manoli?"

"It's a bad habit of mine....calm yourself. Don't burn yourself to death."

"Are you worried about me?"

"Of course. The barrels don't matter as far as I'm concerned, but you're a living person...."

"You bloody liar, Manoli. Ask the policemen around you. They'll tell you...."

All this time, the police had been working fast. They evacuated the house which had the tavern on its ground floor and got in touch with the owners of the shops next to the tavern who sold wood, paint, and odds and ends; people who worked in this street which was now threatened with imminent destruction. Soon, fire engines arrived on the scene and started making preparations. Ahmad Inaba cackled to himself for a long time. "I've got the match in my hand, Manoli!" he yelled.

"I've done nothing wrong," Manoli replied dejectedly. "Calm down,...."

"I've drunk five bottles in honour of your going to Hell...."

"Drink a sixth one, but don't burn yourself...."

The idea pleased him. He stretched out his hand to the shelf, then started drinking again. He felt this was his last chance to really enjoy himself. Suddenly the noise died down.

"Ahmad!" said a gentle voice. Oh dear! There was no mistaking that deep voice.

"Captain?"

"Yes...."

"Welcome...."

"You must be sensible and let us open the door...."

"Why?"

"So that the owner can have it back...."

"A tavern should belong to drinkers!"

"What about me?"

"You'll come out safe and sound...."

"But what about afterwards?"

"Absolutely nothing...."

"Even you're a liar like Manoli!"

"You'll be asked why you were in the tavern, but it's clear that you were so drunk that you fell asleep. You lost consciousness. That's not your fault...."

"What about the broken drawers?"

"You did it unconsciously; you were under the influence...."

"I know what you'll do; the cuffing and beating, the abuse, the imprisonment?!"

"No, no. I promise you'll get the very best treatment."

He almost completely emptied the bottle. "Ahmad Inaba," he shouted, "Sultan of the Turks and Persians. You're all rubbish."

"God forgive you...."

"Do you remember the day my donkey pissed in front of the station as you were coming out?"

"I didn't do a thing...."

"Not to the donkey you didn't; but you slapped my face...."

"I was only joking...."

"Now it's my turn to have a joke!"

"But don't kill yourself."

"Myself? Are you really worried about me?"

"Of course I am. I'm also worried about these people's safety and the shops as well...."

"But you fear God...."

"You don't!"

"You hate hurting other people."

"And you love it...."

"God forgive you."

He finished off the rest of the bottle, and then started

singing: "How I used to lament in love."

"Fantastic, old chap!" the Captain said when he finished the first phrase. "Now maybe you'll come back to your senses."

"I've just finished the sixth bottle!" he replied with a jeer.

"You'll kill yourself...."

"Listen. One last word...."

"Yes?"

"Say: 'I'm a woman'...."

"That won't satisfy you...."

"It will satisfy me completely. That's my condition for allowing you to open the door...."

"I'm a woman!" yelled Manoli.

"You always were a woman, Manoli, without any conditions. But now the Captain has to say it too...."

"Ahmad, you should be ashamed...."

He let out a long guffaw. "By my life, shout it out...." he yelled adamantly.

There was a minute of silence. Then the young men and people standing around let out a storm of shouts: "Long live Ahmad Inaba!" The shouting continued. He leapt to the tavern floor, and started dancing around in arrogant delight in the confined empty space. Everything began to spin with him; chairs, tables, ceiling, and the whole world with them. Suddenly, before he even realized it, the door was opened and the policemen poured in. He stood there tottering while they grabbed hold of his *gallabiyya*, arms and neck. In spite of all that, however, he gave them all an arrogant authoritarian look which seemed to come down from the very heavens. "I haven't got a match on me...." he told them in a heavy sleepy voice which sounded as though it had been recorded at a slow speed.

The Barman

Whatever may have been the case, your face was always there at the happiest moments of my life. There you would be; your left elbow and right palm would be leaning on the white marble table, and you would be looking and waiting, and always smiling. From time to time, you would take a large yellow cloth and wipe the top smoothly. Then you would go back to your place. Behind you wine bottles of all sorts were arranged on four shelves; there they nestled drowsily, full of golden, brown and red liquids. There was no resemblance or point of comparison between their calm, gentle appearance and what lay behind that exterior, full of latent, impulsive forces. Your big round head, your hair parted down the middle, your thick widely-spaced eyebrows, your bushy moustache which curved like a bow, your strong broad chin, your large twinkling blue eyes, and your curved nose, all these things were lines in an unforgettable picture. You were really the king in the cafe-bar Africa.

Sometimes, we would leave our offices in the ministry and slink over to Africa to have a few cups of coffee. We would talk about you quite often without your realizing it.

"How do they choose the barman?" I once asked my fellow civil servants.

"Maybe he began as a waiter," a friend with some experience replied, regarding you with admiration, "But he's chosen with extreme care."

"They command excellent salaries,..." said a second person.

"His knowledge of the human soul is quite remarkable...."

"He's a professor of general knowledge in the fullest sense of the word."

"That's why long-time regulars are the barman's customers before anything else...."

"He's everything. Everything about him is unusual even his name. Vasiliadis...Vasiliadis...just listen to the way it falls on the ear!"

I looked at the barman in admiration, the kind which only young people can feel. His affection was something I really valued, and so I was overjoyed every time he greeted me with a warm, beaming smile which made all my anxieties vanish. On the evening of the weekly day-off, my young age would summon me to him before the evening really began. And what an evening! I had hardly sat down on the tall chair before he would stretch his hand out towards the Dewar's and pour it out for me into the curved glass. He would follow my actions as I drank it down. "Where are you going this evening?" he would ask anxiously.

I would reply that I was going to a cinema, theatre or else some night club or other.

"All that's fine when you're young," he would comment.

"When you're young...." I used to reply with a laugh. "Why this perpetual glorification of youth? Doesn't every stage of life have it's own value?"

"You're attacking youth because you're young. But think carefully about the value of that treasure you have inside your heart...."

"Don't exaggerate, Vasiliadis! Life isn't just blood, or hours and minutes...."

"What is it, then?"

"Above all, Vasiliadis, it's money."

"Money's very important, but youth is more important still. Your appearance shows...."

"Forget about my appearance," I interrupted. "What do you know about a minor official in that accursed ministry of which you can see the entrance from your place behind the bar? We can't always afford what we really want, so please don't talk to me about youth...."

"Do you know how the owner of this cafe fared when he emigrated to Egypt?"

"He was poor and destitute, but then he made his way in a world different from that of ministries and positions. All promotions and raises are blocked indefinitely. So what's left for young people?"

"What's blocked today will be moving again tomorow. Nothing stays as it is. Come on and drink some more...."

He would fill my glass again, and soon I would begin to believe him and approve of his logic. Then, feeling fortified, I would bid him an affectionate farewell.

One festival morning, I returned from the cemetery* to find an invitation from Vasiliadis. I was utterly delighted. "This is a day for drinking, flowers and fine thoughts...." I said as I sat down in front of him that evening.

He filled my glass, and gave me a carnation and a smile. Everything seemed rosy, so much that I even forgot Vasiliadis himself and began to repeat a line of poetry to myself in a low voice, "'You've concealed your love till it hurts; people have blamed you for it, but they're cruel'."

"Poetry?" he asked.

"Yes," I replied, laughing at my complete indifference to what I was doing.

"Tell me what it means."

I was delighted to explain to him word by word. He listened to me with a smile. "Very fine," he said. "But are you a lover or a poet?"

"A lover!" I replied in a tone of confession.

"Fine! But why are you hiding it and why is it cruel?"

"That's the way love is in our country."

"Love means talking freely, loving and being merry

---

*It is the custom in Egypt to visit the graves of one's relatives on certain festival days.

with the one you love..."

"That's the way the Greeks do it."

"And the Romans, everyone...."

"Rule the world, Vasiliadis!" I yelled sarcastically.

"You're strong and well-educated. Any girl would fall in love with you. But don't keep it hidden, or else how can your lover know that you love her? Don't worry if cruel people blame you....drink up!"

He filled my glass up again, and then I believed in what he said. My lost confidence came back, and I left with a heart full of gratitude.

The days went by, but your hair didn't get white, Vasiliadis, nor did the twinkle in your eye fade away.

"How do you keep your youthful appearance?" I asked him one night looking at him in amazement.

"By having friends like you!" he answered with an intelligent smile.

"Your conversation is always delightful," I said taking a glass.

"How's your son?" he asked sympathetically.

"He's getting better. It looks as though there's another one on the way!"

"Congratulations. This is the time to have children. You're a respectable man, and the only thing against you is that you complain too much!"

"Life isn't too good, if the truth be told...."

"How can that be so when you're a respectable civil servant and have a wife and child?"

"I'm talking about our country and political life. but then, maybe you don't bother much about such things."

"Only from a distance. From my position here, I often see demonstrations and hear people yelling. Then I notice the police chasing students. Lorries, ambulances arrive....it often happens. Why are you all so nervous?"

"It's a miserable country, Vasiliadis."

"That's the way politics is in every country. In my own country, Greece, for example, blood has flowed in profusion.

Don't be unhappy about it. Just think about your own position; where were you yesterday and where are you to-day? You'll drink a toast to future victories and I'll remind you....drink up...."

He filled up my glass again. The frown disappeared from my face, and for no obvious reason I felt happy. I left him, thanking God as I did so for our everlasting friendship.

As the days went by, I admired his energy more and more. I used to steal inquisitive looks at him, but never saw the slightest sign of old age. There were his eyes, shining like crystal without ever dimming. Where did he get his fresh supplies of energy?

"Do you drink a lot, Vasiliadis?" I asked.

"No, my friend, just one glass before lunch."

"What about dinner?"

"That consists of yoghurt, lettuce and an apple."

"Don't you ever have any worries?"

"Yes, like everyone else; but I don't give in to them like most people!"

He noticed that I had left my usual place and taken a seat behind the screen which divided the cafe from the drinking corner.

"I notice you prefer to remain out of sight," he said.

"My son is a youngster these days, and I've already seen him with some of his friends passing by the front of the cafe...."

"How strange for a father to be afraid of his own son!"

"My sons cause me a lot of trouble."

"Why? You're a good man."

"We can hardly agree on anything: views or taste. I really feel I'm a stranger."

"Why do you want them to be like you?"

"In our day...."

"You mean, when all promotions and raises were block-ed!" he interrupted.

I couldn't help laughing.

"Then you're not worried by your sons' recalcitrant

attitude!" I said.

"Learn from them, if you can....come on, drink up...."

I raised my glass. "To rebellion and sedition!" I yelled.

Even though we are the very last people to realize the effect which time is having on us, unconcealable signs made it clear to me how much I had changed. Even so, I noticed hardly any change in Vasiliadis. One evening, I went to see him. He stared at me pensively, and I knew why very well.

"You aren't your usual self," he said as soon as he had poured my glass.

"I was pensioned off yesterday," I replied lowering my eyes.

"Bravo!" he replied with a gesture of his hand.

"Why the congratulations, Vasiliadis?"

"You've just successfully completed one stage in your life and now you're beginning another...."

"Which one is that?"

"Life begins at sixty...."

"In the Africa cafe?!"

"Up till now, you've been dealing with the details of life," he replied, shaking his head. "Now it's time to deal with its essence...."

"The truth is that I've found out I'm nothing!"

"You said the same thing about youth one day long ago...."

"I've only got my wife now. If my sons didn't feel it was an obligation, they wouldn't come to visit me!"

"Just concern yourself with one thing, how to enjoy life after sixty."

"But is there anything left in life....?"

"The old life is over, but the new one hasn't begun yet."

"Sometimes I feel giddy," I replied feeling depressed. "It seems to me that everything's just nothing."

"You're in good health and you've got friends. Life in our country doesn't move along quite so monotonously any more."

"I feel a profound sadness inside me which is just

waiting for the chance to break the surface."

"But it can't rub out the happy experiences of your past or your present life."

"The trouble is that you only speak honeyed words."

"There are many days ahead when we can meet, chat and be friends."

"As God wills...."

"Go and visit the zoo, the aquarium and the monuments... Drink up...."

He filled up my glass. What a treasure this Vasiliadis was, I told myself in amazement.

One day, as I was preparing to see in the month of *Ramadan*,* I fell ill with liver disease. My sons came to see me. My friends came too. We passed the time talking about diseases and politics. One morning my wife came in to announce that a *Khwaga*** wanted to see me. Just one minute later, Vasiliadis was embracing me warmly and his wiry moustache was scratching against the edge of my mouth and cheek. For the first time, I was seeing him in a suit and hat.

"The bar's so deserted without the sound of your laughter...," he said with a laugh.

"It's liver disease, God protect you, Vasiliadis!" I replied, feeling the bottom of my back.

"That's a stupid joke, but it'll soon be over. I have to admit that, without you, Vasiliadis is worth nothing."

"And what am I without you, my friend?"

"When are you coming back?"

"At the end of the week perhaps. Where, 0 where is my youth?!"

"I said it was a stupid joke. Then we'll carry on with our good life...."

The truth is that his visit did more for my spirit than even my own sons'. The night I returned to Africa, we

* Ramadan: the fasting month in Islam.
**Khwaga: a foreigner living in Egypt.

embraced in front of everyone.

"To Vasiliadis' health," I said raising my glass, "the symbol of love and loyalty!"

I told him about a dream I'd had in which Death came to visit me.

"Don't believe it," he replied. "Death only comes once, and when it does, it's followed by the greatest happiness of all."

"Now, here you are talking about what comes after death...."

"Where did you come from?" he asked confidently. "Isn't the darkness you came from just like the dark you'll be going to after a long life? It was possible for life to emerge from primeval darkness, so what's to prevent it from continuing in darkness again?!"

"Bravo, Vasiliadis," I yelled drunkenly. "You're the voice of the Saints...."

I went on a big tour round the gardens and monuments and sat under the sun's glowing rays in the desert. But nothing stopped the inevitable from happening. I stayed away from existence for an unspecified period, and, when I returned to consciousness, I found myself stretched out on a bed as though I were dead. It occurred to me that this was the end, but my attachment to life was not to be belittled.

"Vasiliadis sends you his very best wishes," a friend said when he came to see me.

My eyelids flickered in genuine concern for the first time since my prolonged slumber. "I wonder, does he really know how I am?" I asked.

"Yes. Some friends told him and he was really upset...."

"If the *Khwaga* comes," I told my wife after the friend had left, "show him in immediately...."

I told myself that he was a real miracle; he would renew my life through his incredible magic. Every time the bell rang, my eyelids flickered. But Vasiliadis did not come. I asked myself what was keeping him, but failed to think of a convincing answer. I began to feel confused, and the anxiety of it all wore me out. "Vasiliadis hasn't been to visit me...." I told my friend one day.

"He's terribly busy...." he replied as though he were trying to apologize.

"But he was quick to come and visit me last time I was ill...."

He was silent.

"Tell him I'm annoyed," I said feeling agitated.

He was bound to come now, I told myself, however busy he was. I waited tor a long time in vain. My sadness changed to anger. I told myself that he had only been nice to me because....and when he had heard that the end was near, he had stopped bothering about me. This was how the mean devil showed what a lot of experience he had had in purveying foul lies. How devoted he was to the tricks of a professional.

My friend came to visit me a third time when I was hanging between life and death. He heard me muttering his ringing name sorrowfully. He put his head close to mine. "May Vasiliadis' soul rest in peace...." he said.

"No!!...." I yelled in spite of my weakness.

"That's what we all said," he continued. "We couldn't believe our eyes when we saw him collapse behind the bar. A few seconds earlier, he'd been laughing and chatting, standing there like a statue. But, for God's sake, tell me, how else could a man with a strength like his possibly die except from a knock-out blow?!"

A Dream

A tall, broad family tree, made up of names and personal characteristics, but fruitless. He was a mechanic in the Bast Metal Company; he had seven children, but his daily income was thirty *piastres**. He left his beard as it was, not only to save the cost of having it shaved but also because he was a *Sufi*** and one of the Shaikh's followers. At the end of a hard day's work, he would hurry off to the Al-Kumi mausoleum and sit down with the Shaikh. How noble and wonderful he was; that sea, brimming over with the knowledge of God. He would teach him about secular and religious writings. But when he – the mechanic – returned to his own basement apartment late at night, he would find trouble waiting for him. His wife would be there; time had sharpened her tongue, and her limbs and temper as well. "You don't know, of course, what the children have done or what's happened?"

Good Lord Kumi, do children wreck your peace of mind too? Why doesn't the Shaikh talk about the Saints in their own homes?!

"I give you everything I have. All I've got left are curses."

His anger would get the better of him and his tongue would lose control. Secular and religious writings would all disappear, and then a whole night's effort would be completely wasted.

One morning, he found himself looking at the director

* About $5.00 buying power.
** Sufi: a Muslim mystic.

face to face in the large garage. He greeted him as warmly as his feelings of loyalty would allow and shouted a prayer. "Director, Sir," he said, "I saw you in a dream I must tell you about."

The director did not pay any attention but continued on his way.

◆ ◆ ◆ ◆

What dream did that idiot see?!

Dreams have no meaning any more; there is no longer any security. The company, the banana orchard in Shar- qiyya province, and the Khazandar building have all turned into inherited subjects of suspicion. Political aspirations have evaporated. What dream, you dirty *Sunni**?! The ru- mors going around about property being confiscated leave behind them a long trail of anxiety. Is it not amazing after all that a friend of his should tell him that tomorrow is the time for hope? What hope, my friend?

"Let's be realistic," he points out.

"Hope is realistic too," his friend replies.

"Everything seems to be on the point of collapsing."

"You're being too pessimistic."

"No, I'm not. But I don't know what to do."

"Do what any hounded man does."

"What's that?"

"Don't rely completely on the orchard or the building or the company. You should have a safe at home and keep your jewels and trinkets there...."

"What about the hostile atmosphere all around us?"

"Put your nerves in the fridge!"

He remembered the *Sunni* with annoyance; that wretch who professes kindness while there is really a deep-rooted evil glint in his eye. Then he claims he has seen a dream!

* Sunni: an adherent to the more predominant and orthodox group of Muslims (as opposed to the Shia).

"Let me tell you about a dream I had last night," his friend said suddenly.

He laughed loudly, but of course his friend did not understand what was behind it!

◆ ◆ ◆ ◆

He began to feel sure that the director was avoiding looking at him every time he walked by on his way to his car and silently despised him. He was undoubtedly fed up with him and cursed his very existence. He took his suspicions about the director to his colleague in the garage.

"You're making up groundless fancies," the man said. "I swear to you, he doesn't even know you exist."

He forced himself to believe it. Yes, a total non-existence was better than being something which would make the director angry. He wanted to tell the Shaikh about his fears, but he found himself saying something else.

"Your blessing has reached my son," he told the Shaikh. "He's getting better."

"If a little rich boy had contracted the illness he has," the Shaikh said, "a whole bevy of doctors would have come to look at him. God works his splendor on the poor!"

"Why is a believer always struck down?" he asked.

"Because he won't accept any substitute for paradise," came the fervent reply.

Those night sessions in the mausoleum or the drawing room of the house were a tremendous solace for people with wounded hearts; the Shaikh's words were worth much more than all the things which worldly people regard as happiness and finery. The *nargila** which people who err from the straight and narrow path use to satisfy their desires was rightly regarded in the mausoleum as the source of light and godly wisdom. How nice it was to be loved like the Shaikh, and to have people, even rich people, give you their

* Nargila: water pipe

hearts. Thus he would be given valuable gifts and would receive them with forbearance out of respect for the people who gave them, even though he had no real desire for them.

"Why doesn't he give us some of the things God gives him?" one of the Sufi brothers asked him one day.

"Brother," he replied angrily, "he gives us something which money can't buy...."

◆ ◆ ◆ ◆

The July laws, the July laws*. Everyone was found repeating the same thing, the July laws. He started walking to and fro like a maniac.

"Your health's more valuable than anything else!" his wife told him.

"Do you really appreciate the loss we've suffered?"

"Yes. I'm not an idiot nor am I ignorant. But you've got the company, the building and the orchard...."

"What about the new taxes?"

"Your health is the only thing which can't be replaced"

He looked at her face. It was pale and registered the exact opposite of what she had been saying.

"No one knows when the flood is going to stop," he muttered.

"There's still Our Lord."

It was only after a while that he paid any attention to what she said. The truth had flabbergasted him, but he almost managed a smile in spite of the disasterous situation. He thought about her prolonged gaiety and felt a pain inside him. "There's still Our Lord," he muttered, "yes, he exists. But is he for us or against us?"

"There's not a penny of dirty money in our possession.." she said forcefully.

---

* The 1961 laws confiscating and nationalizing the property of foreigners and rich Egyptians.

He did not believe even that any longer without some reservations. Every day voices were being raised; we are the most evil people, they asserted; robbers running all over the face of the earth. Our intelligence is really trickery; our industry is opportunism; our struggles selfishness; our profit, robbery; our generosity, evil exploitation. How can we believe such stuff!?

Faces smiled, not because of affection but to hide a malicious glee. Sometimes, as he was getting into his car, a voice would filter in through the window, "Things are really turning full circle for the tyrant." It would not have been a good idea to get angry or argue with them, and even worse to think of returning their enmity. The police who had previously been his source of protection were now chasing him. The pillars of the temple of Law were collapsing on top of his head. But how could he do anything but repeat what his wife was saying, "There's still Our Lord!?"

◆ ◆ ◆ ◆

"What a day!" he told the Shaikh, his voice shaking with joy.

"Let's begin our studies...." said the Shaikh affectionately.

"But the soul...I mean, we must talk."

"Let's leave creation to its Creator, and proceed on our *Sufi* path."

"The world's changing, master...anyone who used to think...."

"Don't you want to hear some of the things our master Al-Khidr said?"

He found his wife to be a better listener. "They've taken the money away from the rich!" he told her.

The stupid woman did not understand me. "Didn't God give them the money?" she asked.

He gave an angry gesture.

"What are they giving the poor?" she asked. The woman obviously did not want to share in his happiness. She had seen he was happy, and, as usual, had decided to spoil it all for him. He had heard about how terrible the director had looked as he was getting into his car; it had been seen but he had missed seeing it for himself. The man was not out of his mind for long. He found his friend bursting with enthusiasm. When he saw him, he came over. "When there's an earthquake...."

"What's that you're saying, my friend?"

"I'm saying that, when the end comes...." He was about to repeat his wife's question and ask what they were giving to the poor, but he could not work up the courage. The reports about labor salary increments came down rapidly from the heavens. Yes, my friend, son of Our Father, we are being created afresh.

"Listen to me," the Shaikh said. He wanted to listen, but his mind was brimming over with emotion.

"Make sure you don't show any malice...." the Shaikh warned.

He replied that he did not feel any malice towards any-one and he did not have any enemies. But in spite of that, he still looked drunk with happiness.

"You're sliding back down the path...." the Shaikh told him.

He closed his eyes to blot out the world which was jar-ring his nerves so much.

"Ask God's forgiveness...." the Shaikh said.

"But I haven't done anything wrong, master," he repli-ed. "After all, the Qur'an talks of the joy of life being in mo-ney and children, doesn't it?"

He sat up straight as a preparation for hearing what the Shaikh had to say, but instead he heard, "You're beyond my reach!"

◆ ◆ ◆ ◆

That *Sunni!* Whenever I pass by, he insists on greeting

me in a tone of voice like some chanter or other! He did not look any different from all the rest of them, but he had his own special evil ways. It would not be long, he thought, before he would be surprising him with some new dream. Why do I keep on bothering myself with him as though he were the one and only unpleasant thing in the world? Sorrow is treading all over my friends like a disease. But I must resist, they say, not care...and other phrases like these which do not have any meaning any more. His wife makes a big display of being happy, especially at the club; the walls ring with the sound of laughter all night, maniacs' laughter. In spite of that, they are saying that we have fallen into a big trap where there is still some room to move. But he is a tough nut to crack and he will not break or soften. Now he is falling into another trap of his own making. Yes, he decided to have a passionate affair with the German dancer at the Continental night-club. It was her aloofness which excited him more than her blonde hair.

"We were and still are the Elite!" she told him during the course of a long conversation.

"I love your sadness as much as I love you," he replied emotionally.

She was as sharp as an arrowhead, but it was hidden beneath a silken wrapping. His wife meanwhile fell by the wayside in spite of her artificial happiness. He felt sorry for her, but the love that he felt for her moved rapidly to an unexpected death. And when the company was nationalized, everything moved in the direction of death. His wife told him to hurry up and sell the orchard and building. That was an idea, but who would buy them? And where would they put the money?

"The best thing we can do is to do nothing," he said.

He gave himself up entirely to his passionate love affair. Biological and physiological elements were combining to destroy him from the inside, he told himself, so it was not right to reinforce them with some deliberate misery of his own making through his external behavior.

The *Sunni* came to his mind one morning as he was shaving. "What dream, you lecher!?" he muttered.

◆ ◆ ◆ ◆

"Are you really listening to me?" the Shaikh asked him.

"Yes, master...." he replied timidly, feeling confused. He looked at him sorrowfully.

"You're not coming regularly," he said.

"To tell you the truth...."

"The world has seduced you away...."

"Never. I'm looking for an apartment somewhere on the earth's surface."

The Shaikh seemed unusually languid. The man hoped and prayed that the languor was not the result of his not giving him any more gifts because of his changed circumstances. "Raises and sharing in the profits," said the Shaikh. "What do you do with the blessings God showers on you?"

"The same as a thirsty person does when he discovers a cup of water!"

"But the world can never satisfy anyone who seeks it...."

"I've only asked for my essential needs to be satisfied...."

"Life in this world has led you astray."

"Never. God is my witness...."

"I'm telling you that life in this world has led you astray...."

For a moment, there was silence. "Is there any harm," the man asked cautiously, "in nominating myself for the administrative council?"

"Administrative council!"

"It's useful work. My colleagues think highly of me...."

"It's no good asking a *Sufi* about that...."

"A sincere man once said that there's as much worship in life as there is in seclusion...."

"All that's left for you to do is to shave your beard," the Shaikh said lowering his eyes.

There was another silence.

◆ ◆ ◆ ◆

"We haven't suffered too badly compared with some of the others."

He asked his friend what he meant. "Sequestration, for example," his friend replied tersely.

"Who knows what may happen tomorrow?"

They looked at each other for a long time.

"What have we done wrong?" he asked his friend.

"History's full of bloody events...."

"Sometimes I almost believe what they say about our crimes!"

His friend gave him a quizzical look. "If it's not so," he continued, "then why has God washed his hands of us?"

He plunged into his passionate love affair right up to his ears. His wife's condition went from bad to worse. One morning, he read the *Sunni's* name among the list of people who had been elected in the administrative council elections. "The lecherous devil with the dream!" he yelled angrily.

He stopped reading newspapers. He was amazed at his friend's excessive gaiety in spite of the losses which he was suffering on all sides.

"You're playing an inappropriate role," he told him.

"It's true we've been robbed of our money," his friend replied with a loud laugh. "But shall I show you the man who gave away countless money without having it stolen from him?"

He started thinking of all his friends who were Pashas or Beys, but his friend anticipated his reply. "His name is Gautama Buddha!" he said. With a gesture of his pipe, he urged him to listen. "I'll tell you the incredible story about him...." he continued.

Passers—by

The enormous street was a part of these people's lives: Qasr an-Nil Street. Every morning, they would walk down it between seven and eight and then branch off to their various places of work. As the years went by, the same journey would be repeated with a cosmic regularity. Many of them started doing it when they were still in the prime of their youth and would keep it up until old age caught up with them and they could feel the end approaching. Some of them would disappear for reasons which remained undisclosed, since they never introduced themselves, even though they all shared the walk down the street with each other. They would look around, but their eyes took hardly anything in; it was as if the other people were trees planted on the sidewalk. Occasionally, something would make them wake up, and then they would look in amazement at the strange world passing by on its way. Each and every person was a little world of his own, made up of secrets, joys and sorrows. It knew nothing of other people; there was no time for it to get to know itself, and it had not the slightest idea of its own destiny. At that point, there would be an exhausting quest for answers but they were in short supply until there was some pressure. The sky, clear or overcast according to the season, turned its nose up at the whole thing without offering any satisfaction or dispelling the feeling of bewilderment. Three people persevered with this daily journey, two Egyptian men and a European woman. The men began it in about 1925, and the woman appeared some years later. They were all young in those days. One of the men was tall and thin; he was distinguished by his piercing eyes, his dark complexion and nervous movements. The other one was of medium height and stature, and had a gentle disposition. The woman was a real beauty with her blue eyes and black hair, her complexion was milky white and she had a slender figure. She and the tall young man used to walk in the direction of Opera Square while the other man walked towards Sulaiman Pasha Square. They would usually meet midway down the street or thereabouts. Neither of the men would miss the opportunity provided by the encounter to take a look at the girl. The young man of medium height would look at her shyly, merely wanting to brighten up his day, the other would devour her greedily with his piercing eyes. It was not just a look; he was speaking, acting, leering lecherously. He was seen once calling to her, but she avoided him and ran away from him as fast as she could. She seemed to be serious and energetic with all the determination and single-mindedness of a working girl. She hardly ever looked at anything apart from the road she was walking along. If ever her eyes met those of the young man of medium height, it was only enough to satisfy an enquiring mind; the kind of normal exchange between two pedestrians on the very lowest level. The shy young man began to look angrily at the other man and followed his dallying escapades with an anxious concern and annoyance. He expected to see him any morning with the young girl on his arm. The more he cursed his rival's brazen conduct, the more he began to admire her secretly himself. Deep down inside of him he wanted part of her for himself. It made him feel very unhappy that the other two went one way and that he went the other way.

And so these three stars continued on their courses without the slightest change in their communal relations towards each other. Each one of them acted independently as wedding rings gradually appeared on their fingers. The man of medium height was the first, and the tall man followed him at the end of the same year. The lovely girl caught up with them in the end. But even so, there did not seem to be any great diminution in the feelings of love for her even though it seemed that the tall man had got rid of his amorous dreams almost completely.

When the second world war started, nothing changed between the three of them even though the whole world plunged headlong towards the most momentous changes. The newspapers were regaled with headlines telling of bloody battles and passers-by spread the stunning news around. English civilians began to appear in large numbers even at this early hour. Three bars were opened on this venerable street. The onslaught of change touched the girl herself as an example of the world around her. Her walk became heavier and she grew pale. Then her stomach began to bulge and spread out underneath the traditional loose garment without a belt. Yes, the fascinating bride was pregnant. The tall man watched her like a hawk. He felt annoyed as he thought of his own wife, but his eyes were full of kindness and a weird feeling of distraction. She was pregnant a second time before the end of the war and a third time during the Palestine war of 1948. Maybe one of the three was only really aware of time when he looked at the other. The woman's figure began to fill out, and all memory of that girl with the gorgeous curvaceous body faded away. Her eyes were surrounded by semi-circles which could not be hidden any longer. She had a poised look about her, a poise induced by the burdens of life, not the kind of spoiled and discouraging poise they had known before. The tall man had changed completely; white hair invaded his sideburns and moustache, and the bones on his cheeks jutted out. And even though the man of medium height had not noticed any change in himself except for his grey hair, he had no doubts how much he had really changed when he looked at his two companions. He felt a tension deep down inside him as though it were a far-off echo of what happened in history and on the road around him.

The three stars continued in their course through the new series of events. Bitter fighting had started at the

Canal*, then the Cairo fire started**, and finally the July revolution*** burst into the open. Society was shaken to its foundations, and the tottering structure collapsed. The new system began to crystalize, but then the threefold attack of 1956 blocked the path like a blind bull. During the invasion, fate willed that these three people should meet in one place for the first time. The air raid siren went off and gunfire started as they were walking in front of the Lagiyun bar. The three of them took shelter inside the bar in a spontaneous rush and found a servant inside washing the floor. There was only one table available for them to sit at and it was in the far corner. They made towards it through stacks of chairs piled one on top of the other and stood there, hesitating, anxious.... Then at the servant's invitation they sat down around the solitary table. Every time there was an explosion, they looked at each other indifferently without saying a word. The tall man was the first to dare to break the wall of silence. "Not even like the World War...." he said.

"Criminals!" the other man said. "They soon forget how humiliated they were by Hitler!"

The conversation carried on in this vein, but the woman did not take part in it. The shooting slackened off somewhat.

"There's no need to be afraid," the tall man continued. "They're aiming at targets."

The woman looked at him in a way which showed that she was hankering for confirmation of what he had just said. He smiled at her. From close up, she looked at the very peak of feminine maturity even though her good looks seemed about to desert her.

"The best thing we can do," said the tall man, stimulated by a sudden burst of joviality, "is to forget what's going on outside." He smiled and showed a fine set of teeth.

* January, 1952
** January 26, 1952
*** July 23, 1952

"We've met every morning for a very long time. It's like a dream...."

The other man thought for a moment. "Since 1925," he said.

The tall man looked at Madame. "You appeared on the scene later, didn't you, Madame?" he asked.

She had been concentrating on what was happening outside with a good deal of alarm, but shook herself out of it and nodded in reply.

"A long life has gone by without our exchanging a single word!" he continued with a laugh. "That's why I'm not surprised when two or three nations fight each other!"

"When's the shooting going to stop?" the woman asked herself tensely.

"Don't worry, Madame," he said in an affectionate voice. "The firing will soon be over, and each one of us will go his own way. But I'd like to take this opportunity to put into practice a marvellous idea which has only just occurred to me!"

The man of medium height looked at him with an unenthusiastic curiosity while the woman looked at her watch.

"In a month's time, I'm being pensioned off," he said. "In other words, I shall no longer see either of you after our long and dear relationship...."

"It's the same with me," the other man said. "I shall be retiring at the end of this year."

"This means that we should certainly carry out my idea. Why don't we celebrate the memory of more than thirty years of our long acquaintance!?"

He looked at them both enthusiastically. Outside, it began to get quiet bit by bit although the all-clear siren had not sounded yet.

"I'd like to invite you both to a light supper at the Chrysantheme restaurant by the Pyramids. What do you think, Sir?"

"I'd be delighted if I have the time," the other man replied in a negative tone.

"If Madame accepts, I'm sure you'll regard it as a special obligation to accept. What do you think, Madame?"

Once again, she shook herself out of her panicky feelings. "I...." she muttered.

"No hesitation," he interrupted. "There's no harm in it at all. My invitation is quite obviously well-intentioned. It wouldn't be humane of you to turn it down...."

She gave a slight smile. and he interpreted that as an acceptance. "Thank you," he said quickly. "We'll work out the exact day some morning in the near future...."

They made arrangements on the third morning after the fighting stopped. They met in Tahrir Square and took a taxi out to Chrysantheme. They got there before sunset. They spent this time introducing themselves. The tall man introduced himself as Ali Baraka, a translator; the other man as Sayyid Izzat, accounts director; and Madame Mathias, a tailoress in the shop *My Star*. They sat down in a private room which was kept hidden from the rest of the place by a door which was ajar and had a screen behind it. Ali Baraka ordered pigeon and liver* for dinner and asked for some cognac. He looked at Sayyid Izzat and raised his glass. "Let's drink to the youth of 1925," he said. "Of course, Madame, you are still young!"

"No, no; there's no point in lying," she replied with a laugh. "You know that as well as he does."

They had hardly emptied the glasses before fresh ones were ordered.

"Don't say no," he said. "Let's drink; we won't get drunk at any rate. This is the night of our lives."

Familiarity took the place of reserve. The effect of the cognac coupled with Ali Baraka's smooth manner and energy gave them a feeling of warmth.

"We should have been great friends," he said, "the kind of people who share their secrets with each other. But unfortunately, it's too late now. To make our introductions

---

* Both are expensive in Egypt.

absolutely complete, the only thing we can do is to remember some of the really essential things which happened to us. For example, what was the happiest moment in our lives, or what had the greatest effect on us?"

Sayyid Izzat welcomed the suggestion for the simple reason that he could not think of anything else to say. "I suppose the happiest thing which happened to me," he said, "was when my eldest son passed his secondary certificate when he seemed a hopeless case...."

He looked expectantly at Madame as though she were the real reason for his making this suggestion. "My eldest daughter's marriage," she said with a smile. "But the thing which I'll never forget is my husband's death four years ago."

He almost let slip a gesture of delight, but managed to cover it with a fake frown of concern and then shook his head sorrowfully. Seizing the opportunity of the silence which followed her answer, he asked for a third round of cognac. Then he laughed as he opened a new page. "The things which happened to me are slightly peculiar," he said. "The happiest was when a relative died and left me all his money, and the unhappiest was caused by you, Madame!"

"Me?"

"Yes, and you know why."

The cognac had its own latent effect on her, and she felt urged to reply. "You mean chasing after me in the street?"

"I mean that you avoided me even before you were married."

"My dear man, you weren't serious...."

"How did you know?"

"I understand these things. You weren't serious...."

"I agree," said Sayyid Izzat emptying his glass.

"You as well! Did I keep my good intentions hidden to this extent?"

"You didn't have any good intentions!"

"And what about you!? You used to tear her clothes off with your eyes!"

"I don't deny it!" Sayyid Izzat admitted. Ali Baraka laughed maliciously.

"I don't believe it," said Madame Mathias.

"Why?"

Dinner came along with another round of cognac. They started eating. The question hung there in mid-air while concern about the answer stretched away into infinity.

"I've something to tell you," said Madame Mathias whose ears had turned red from all the drinking.

"Me?" asked Sayyid Izzat.

"You used to look at me so hard, every morning. I told myself that one day you were bound to speak to me!"

"I thought you didn't notice anything at all!"

"Ha! I told myself that you would speak to me. The only thing holding you back, I thought, was that you were being excessively formal as opposed to...."

Ali Baraka interrupted with a loud laugh. "As opposed to the other boorish man!" he shouted.

"No, no, excuse me...." she said with a laugh. Then she looked at Sayyid again. "I thought the whole thing was settled," she said, "so settled in fact that I told Mother about it, but she was utterly opposed to the idea of my marrying an Egyptian."

Sayyid Izzat was enjoying the conversation so much that he forgot about his food. "Marriage?" he shouted.

"Yes...I got angry with Mother over you and went to stay with my aunt for a while...."

Sayyid smiled in embarrassment and delight as he should have done in 1930.

"You lost your chance and spoiled mine too," said Ali Baraka punching him on the arm. "Whoever it was who said that accountants are complicated to the very end was right!"

"I didn't realize!" Sayyid Izzat muttered. "Madame, you were so serious and it was most discouraging."

"That's the advice which my friend gave me once in *My Star*. She was a Jewess born in Egypt. She told me that Egyptians like playgirls, but they only marry women who are reserved!"

"Marvellous Jewish advice!" Ali Baraka yelled, his mouth stuffed full of pigeon.

"But you never said anything," said Madame to Sayyid Izzat, "you didn't even try to say a word."

"I was always afraid of Europeans.", he replied in embarrassment.

"Afraid?"

"Yes. Something told me that you were out of reach because you were European. Every time I thought of saying something, I was so afraid that my tongue stuck in my mouth."

"Of course, I understand," said Ali Baraka scoffing with laughter. "The financial regulations didn't permit love between an Egyptian and a European."

"My salary was limited, and in those days I thought love was a heavy drain on expenses!"

"I waited and waited till I felt ashamed of myself," Madame said with a shrug of her shoulders. "That was when I met Monsieur Mathias.."

"You waited for the silent one," said Ali Baraka reproachfully, "and resisted all the eloquent speaker's advances!?"

Dinner came to an end but the drinking did not. Signs of it could be seen in their cheeks, eyes and tongues. The laughter got louder.

"I've got an idea!" Ali Baraka shouted with the tone of voice of someone who is about to make a welcome suggestion. They both looked at him enquiringly.

"Let's dance!"

"I don't know how to," Sayyid Izzat said.

"There isn't any music," Madame said.

"No matter," replied Ali Baraka, and then offered her his arm. She stood up in compliance. He put his arm round her waist, and they started dancing. Then he clutched her to him till they were in complete contact with each other. She tried to get away from him but in vain.

"What kind of dancing is this?!" Sayyid Izzat asked in confusion.

"Please...if you don't mind...." said Madama exhausted.

But Ali Baraka carried on with a terrifying look in his eye.

"Be careful!" Sayyid yelled, "Madame is tired...."

"No one will know us here!" was the angry reply.

"Get away...leave me alone...." said Madame pushing him away weakly.

Sayyid Izzat got up. The way he stood up showed that he was really drunk. He put his hand on the tall man's shoulder. "Ali Bey," he begged, "be reasonable, don't disgrace us!"

"Be reasonable yourself," Ali Baraka replied, jerking his hand off with a movement of his shoulder. "Your turn will come, you fool!"

She moaned in pain.

"Let her go," yelled Sayyid angrily, "I'm telling you to let her go. Can't you understand?"

He grabbed him by the arms and tried to separate them. He pulled them with all the strength he could muster. The woman was squeezed in between them till he could feel her soft body. He moved back a step and doubled his efforts. He felt a searing sense of shame and disgrace.

"Go away or else...." Ali Baraka yelled.

"You'll disgrace us!"

"I'll scream," yelled Madame, "I'm telling you, I'll scream!"

Sayyid Izzat moved round to the other side till he was behind Ali Baraka. He grabbed hold of him by the neck and tightened his hold mercilessly till he almost strangled him. Then he stepped back in a state of collapse. Madame groaned and fell back into a chair with her eyes closed. All you could hear was them gasping for breath. Each one of them retired into himself, nursing his own wounds. Madame looked as though she were asleep, Ali Baraka was leaning against the wall and Sayyid felt sick and was screwing up his face in pain.

"I'm not paying anyone's bill!" said Ali Baraka angrily.

Madame stretched out her hand towards her handbag, but Sayyid Izzat seized it gently. "No one will be paying for us," he said.

Silence reigned again. They all felt exhausted. Then Sayyid had an idea. He called for the waiter and ordered two glasses of cognac. Before the waiter disappeared behind the screen, Ali Baraka asked him for a third glass. This time they drank it as though they were taking some medicine, silently and without any sign of gaiety. Ali Baraka started pacing up and down the room and then went out. After a few minutes he came back; his face looked washed and his features looked relaxed. "I've paid the whole bill...." he said looking at them both.

"No!" Sayyid Izzat protested.

"It's been paid, and that's the end of it!" Ali Baraka said, and then carried on in a gentler tone of voice. "Let's forget what happened. That's the best thing we can do."

He smiled almost apologetically. He went up to Sayyid. "Lean forward!" he said. He kissed him on the forehead before the other man could realize what he intended to do. Then he went over to Madame and muttered the same thing. He kissed her forehead without any resistance from her. "I'm sorry, Madame," he said with his head still level with hers, "peace is best!" Then suddenly he kissed her on the mouth. After that, he stood up and moved back. "The kiss of peace," he said, "in salute to an old dream which I had before Saad Zaghlul's death*!"

They left the restaurant. He took her right hand and let the other man take her left. The three of them walked outside; it was slightly chilly. The moon was hidden behind some silvery clouds. The desert stretched out into the darkness all the way to the distant lights shining like a

* The famous Egyptian Nationalist leader who died in 1927.

necklace of stars on the Muqattam Hills.

"Let's think of a nice song all three of us know," said Ali Baraka with a laugh, "and we'll sing it together."

The Black Cat Tavern

They were all singing a song when a strange man appeared at the door.

There was not an empty seat left in the tavern. It – the tavern – consists of a square room at the bottom of an old, dilapidated building. As the surroundings in which it is buried are very dark, it has to be lit day and night. A single window looks out on a back alley through some iron bars. The walls are painted a light blue colour and give off moisture at various places making dark stains. The door opens out on to a long, narrow passageway which stretches as far as the street. On one side, kegs of hellish wine stand in rows. The customers of this tavern are all one family, with its various branches distributed around the bare wooden tables. Some of them are bound to others by ties of friendship and camaraderie, and they are all bound together by a feeling of brotherhood inspired by the sense of unity which the place gives them and by the spiritual communion which they enjoy together night after night. The evening chatter and hellish wine bring them all together.

They were all singing a song when a strange man appeared at the door.

It often happens that one of them is asked, "Why do you prefer the Black Cat Tavern?"

Its real name is "The Star," but it is usually called the Black Cat Tavern. This is because of the huge black cat which belongs there, the pet of the owner who is Greek, (a lean man of slender build) and friend and good-luck symbol of all the customers.

"I prefer the Black Cat Tavern for its warm family atmosphere, and because for just a *piastre* or two you can fly without having any wings...."

The black cat moves around from table to table after bread crumbs and bits of *ta'miyya* and fish. He steps hesitantly among people's feet and rubs against their legs with all the reckless abandon of someone born with a golden spoon in his mouth. His Greek master leans his elbows on the table and gazes at nothing in particular with a blank stare. The aged waiter takes the wine around or else regularly refills the small cups from the taps on the wine barrels.

"It's the kindest tavern there is for people with a regular income."

People tell each other jokes and strange tales, and they feel drawn closer together by telling each other about their complaints. Someone with a clear voice may sing a song, and then the whole damp, subterranean place will overflow with a feeling of happiness.

"There's nothing wrong with forgetting for an hour that we have big families and little money."

"Or forgetting the heat and the flies...."

"Or forgetting that there's a world beyond the bars...."

"Or in enjoying the black cat's pleasant company."

When they all meet, they feel cheerful and at ease; their hearts overflow with love for everything. Free of all fanaticism and fear, and purged of the spectres of disease, old age and death, they paint an illusory picture of themselves, racing ahead of time by whole centuries.

They were all singing a song when a strange man appeared at the door.

The man looked round the place in every direction and couldn't see an empty table. He disappeared from view into the passageway and everyone thought he had gone for good, but he came back carrying a chair made of interwoven straw – the Greek owner's own chair – put it down close to the narrow door and sat down.

He had been scowling when he first came, he was scowling when he came back again, and he was still scowling when he sat down. He didn't glance at anyone. His eyes looked sharp and severe, but they were far away, finding refuge in some unknown, distant world, without noticing any of the people who filled the small place. His general appearance looked dark, strong and frightening, as though he were a wrestler a boxer, or else someone used to lifting heavy loads. His clothes matched his dark appearance completely and even gave it some emphasis, with the black pullover, dark grey trousers and brown rubber shoes. In this whole dark ensemble, the only thing which shone was the square bald pate which crowned his huge, solid head.

His unexpected arrival released an electric charge which penetrated to the very depths of the people who were sitting around. The singing stopped. The cheerful expressions on people's faces changed. The laughter subsided. They were all of two minds as to whether to look straight at him, or steal glances in his direction. However, this did not last long. After being stunned by the shock of surprise and the alarming scene, they all came to their senses again and refused to let a stranger spoil their evening's enjoyment for them. They made signs at each other to ignore him and resume their fun and games. So they all started chatting, joking and drinking again. But he was never really out of their minds, and they weren't able to ignore him completely; he kept on weighing down their spirits like an aching tooth. Then he clapped his hands with a disarming power, and the old waiter came up to him bringing some of the hellish wine. He quickly emptied the cup and followed it with another. Then he ordered four more cups at one go and started drinking one cup after another till he had finished them all, and then gave the same order again. Everyone started feeling alarmed and worried again; the laughter died away on their lips, and once again they sat there in stunned silence. What kind of man was this?! He had drunk enough of this hellish wine to kill an elephant. Yet here he was, sitting there like a solid piece of stone without reacting in any way or softening his expression.

What kind of man was this?!

The black cat went over to him inquisitively and waited to be thrown something or other. When it didn't feel that its existence was being noticed, it started rubbing against the man's leg. The man stamped the ground with his foot, and the cat sprang back. No doubt it was surprised at being treated in this way; it had never happened before. The Greek owner turned his head in the direction of the room with a lifeless expression on his face. He stared at the stranger for a while, and then went back to looking at nothing.

The stranger now emerged from his inertia. He moved his head violently to right and left, and gritted his teeth. He started talking in an inaudible voice either to himself or else to someone in his imagination. He looked threatening and menacing as he moved his fist up and down. A look of terrible anger was fixed on his face. Silence and fear prevailed over everything. Then his voice was heard for the first time, a coarse voice which sounded like cattle mooing. It reverberated loud and clear with the words, "Curse... woe...." He clenched his fist and continued, "Let the mountain come... and what is beyond it."

For a moment, he was quiet, and then he carried on in a slightly lower tone of voice, "That's the problem, quite simply and frankly stated."

They were all convinced that there was no point in staying any longer; the evening's entertainment had already ended in failure when it had hardly even begun.

They decided to leave peaceably. After exchanging glances with one another, they reached an understanding and made ready to get up and go. At this point, the man noticed them all for the first time. He emerged from his daze, looked them all over enquiringly, and stopped them short with a gesture. "Who are you people?" he asked.

That was a question to be ignored and despised, if ever there was one; but nobody thought of doing so.

"We've been customers here for a long time...." one of them replied, encouraged by his old age.

"When did you come?"

"We came with the evening...."

"You came before I arrived then, did you?"

"Yes."

He signalled to them to return to their seats. "No one will leave," he said in a stern and determined tone of voice.

They could not believe their ears. They were so shocked that their tongues were tied, and yet no one dared to give him the reply he deserved.

"But we want to leave," the old man said in a calm voice which was the complete opposite of the way he really felt.

The man gave them a threatening look like a piece of stone. "Anyone who wants to give up his life can step forward!" he said.

None of them wanted to give up his life. They looked at each other in stunned confusion.

"Why do you want to stop us leaving?" the old man asked.

"Don't you people try to deceive me," he said, shaking his head with a bitter scorn. "You heard everything...."

"I assure you, we didn't hear a thing...." the old man replied in amazement.

"Don't you people try to deceive me," he yelled angrily. "You know the story!"

"We didn't hear a thing, and we don't know a thing either!"

"You deceitful liars!"

"You've got to believe us...."

"Why should I believe a load of noisy drunkards?!"

"You're insulting innocent people and hurting their dignity!"

"Anyone who wants to give up his life can step forward."

It was clear to them all that the situation could only be resolved by force, and they hadn't any of that. So they were compelled to sit down under the influence of his terrifying gaze. They all returned to their seats with a feeling of sup-

pressed anger and humiliation which they had never experienced before.

"How long are we going to stay here?" the old man
asked.

"Till the appropriate time comes."

"And when will that be?"

"Cut your tongue out and wait."

The time passed in an atmosphere of painful tension.
They all felt overcome with anxiety and worry, and the
wine flew right out of their heads. Even the black cat sensed
the smell of hostility in the air and leapt up to the sill of the
solitary window! Once there, it settled down, folded its legs
under its head, and closed its eyes putting its tail in between
the bars. Individual questions preyed on their minds. Who
was this man? Was he drunk? Was he mad? What was the
story he was accusing them of hearing? All this time, the
Greek owner of the tavern maintained his deathly si-lence,
while the waiter kept on serving people as though he
wasn't seeing or hearing anything.

The strange man began to look at them with a scornful
malice. "If any one of you tries any funny business," he said
in a threatening tone of voice, "I'll punish you all without
mercy...."

Now that he had begun to talk again, they felt
encouraged to say something. "I swear to you," the old man
said sincerely, "we all swear to you...."

"What will you swear to me by, if I ask you?" the man
interrupted.

A tiny ray of hope stirred in their hearts. "By anything
you like," the old man replied eagerly, "by our children, God
Almighty!"

"Nothing is of any value to customers of a sordid tavern
like this one!"

"We're not the kind of people you think we are; we're
honest parents and faithful believers. For that reason, we
feel an even greater need to refresh our overburdened
souls...."

"You despicable wretches!" he yelled, his voice echoing around the room. "You dream about building castles without any effort on your part but through some despicable exploitation of *the* story!"

"We swear to you by God Almighty that we know nothing about the story. We've no idea about it...."

"Who among you hasn't got a story, you cowards!"

"But you weren't talking. Your lips were moving, but no sound came out!"

"Don't try to fool me, you windbag...."

"You must believe us and leave us alone...."

"Too bad for anyone who moves and tries any funny business. If anything happens, I'll smash your heads in and use them to make a barricade to block the passageway...."

The man was really terrifying. Maybe he was afraid as well; that would make the outcome twice as bad. Despair began to creep into their hearts like a deathly chill. He kept on drinking, but did not get drunk and showed no signs of flagging or calming down. There he was, blocking the only exit, strong and rugged, made of steel just like the bars in the window.

They started looking at each other hopelessly. Every time they spotted a shape beyond the bars, their hearts flew out to it longingly although they didn't try to move at all. Even the black cat seemed to have deserted them completely and carried on enjoying his sleep. One of them could not hold himself any longer. "Can I go to the toilet?" he asked nervously.

"Who told you I was a wetnurse?" the stranger replied angrily.

"Are we going to stay like this till the morning?" the old man asked with a sigh, "Is that to be our fate?"

"You'll be lucky if the morning ever dawns...." It was absurd to argue; the man was either mad or on the run, or both. Maybe there was a story behind him, and maybe there was nothing. In spite of their number, they were prisoners; he was strong and powerful, while they had neither power nor resolve. But wasn't there any way to resist, whatever type of resistance it might be?

They started looking at each other again. Misery showed clearly in their eyes. They started whispering quietly so that the stranger wouldn't hear.

"What a disaster!"

"What a humiliation!"

"What a disgrace!"

Then suddenly a look which seemed to show something like a smile; no, it really was a smile, wasn't it?

"Why not? The whole situation is terribly funny."

"Funny?"

"Think about it dispassionately for a moment, and you will find it devastatingly funny."

"Really?"

"I'm afraid I'll burst out laughing...."

"Remember," the old man said in a partially audible voice, "there's still a long while to go before the time when we usually break up."

"But there's no time left for any of our usual evening chatter, is there?"

"That's because we let it stop without any reason."

"Without any reason?!"

"I mean, there isn't any reason why we shouldn't carry on with it now."

"In what kind of spirit can we carry on after what's happened?"

"Let's forget the door for a while and see what happens."

No one welcomed the suggestion, but no one rejected it either. The cups of hellish wine reappeared in full view of the strange man, but he paid no attention. They started drinking the wine in excessive amounts. Heads started to reel, and the drink made them feel cheerful again. Anxieties were swept away by some magic wizardry, and laughter began to ring out. They danced on their seats, they exchanged puns, and sang in chorus, "'The day of revelry is coming, coming soon'."

All this time, they ignored the other subject, and forgot about its existence entirely. The black cat woke up and started moving from one table to another and from one leg to another. They drank with a will, they sang with a will and they were crude with a will; it was as though they were enjoying their last night in the tavern.

A miracle occurred. The present receded until it melted into an expanding forgetfulness. Memory disintegrated, throwing out of its cells everything which had been stored away in them. Nobody knew who his companion was. It was the hellish wine really, but... yes indeed... but....

"But where are we?"

"Tell me who we are, and I'll tell you where we are!"

"Was there singing?"

"It was more like weeping as far as I can remember...."

"Was there a story then... I wonder what story?"

"This black cat, it's a tangible object without any doubt."

"Certainly. It's the thread to lead us to the truth...."

"Now we're getting near the truth...."

"This cat was a deity in our forefathers' time."

"One day, he sat at the door of a prison-cell, then announced the secret of the story...."

"And threatened woe."

"But what's the story?"

"Originally it was a deity, then it was changed into a cat...."

"But what's the story?"

"How can a cat talk?"

"Didn't it tell us the story in detail?"

"Yes, but we wasted time weeping and singing."

"Now the threads have been completed, and the way is prepared to discover the truth...."

The old waiter's voice yelled out rebukes and threats at someone or other. "Wake up, you lazy devil," he shouted, "or else I'll smash your head in."

A huge man with his head lowered dejectedly came forward, and started picking up the glasses and dishes, cleaning the tables, and collecting the refuse from the floor. He carried on doing his job without saying a word or looking at anyone. He seemed to be overwhelmed by a feeling of deep sorrow, and his eyes were flowing with tears.

They all followed his movements with feelings of regret and sympathy.

"What's the story?" one of them asked him.

But the man paid no attention to him, and carried on working in silence with the same sad expression on his face and tears in his eyes.

"Where and when have I seen that man?" the old man asked.

The man walked towards the passageway. He was dressed in dark clothes, consisting of a black pullover, dark grey trousers, and brown rubber shoes.

"Where and when have I seen that man?" the old man asked himself again.

Under the Bus Shelter

The grey clouds hung close together and obscured the sky; it was as dark as nightfall. Drizzle began to fall, and a damp, blustery wind blew down the street. Passers-by hurried on their way except for a few who clustered together under the bus-shelter. The very monotony of the scene would have frozen it then and there, but suddenly a man burst out of a side street running like a lunatic and disappeared into another street on the other side. A group of men and boys chased after him yelling, "Thief!... catch the thief." The din gradually died away to nothing, and the drizzle still fell. The street was now empty, or almost so. There were only some people under the bus-shelter waiting for the bus and others who were simply sheltering there for fear of getting wet. The noise of the people chasing the thief started again and got louder as they came closer. Then they came into view. They had caught the thief, and boys were cheering round them with loud, piercing yells. Half way across the road, the thief tried to get away, but they grabbed him and started punching him and beating him up. They hit him so hard that he started fighting back vainly and struck out at them at random. The people under the bus-shelter were watching the struggle closely.

"Aren't they hitting him hard?! They're being very brutal."

"Where's going to be a crime much worse than stealing!"

"Look! The Policeman is just standing there watching...."

"No! He's turned away and is looking in the other

direction...."

It started to drizzle even harder; it came down in silvery streaks, and then rain started to pour down. The street was empty except for the people who were fighting and the others under the bus-shelter. The men got tired and stopped hitting each other. They gathered round the thief out of breath and began to exchange inaudible words with him. They were soon involved in an important discussion which no one else could make out. No one seemed to be caring about the rain; their clothes stuck to their bodies, but they persevered with the discussion without bothering in the least about the rain. The thief's gestures showed clearly that he was defending himself fiercely, but no one believed him. From the way he was gesticulating with his arms, he seemed to be making a speech, but his voice was lost in the distance and in the din of the pouring rain. He was certainly making a big speech, and there was everyone standing in the rain listening to him and staring dumbly. The people under the shelter kept on looking at them. "How is it the policeman isn't moving?!" one of them asked.

"That's why it strikes me the whole thing is a scene from a film!"

"The beating looked real enough...."

"But holding a discussion and making speeches in the rain?!"

Now something else attracted their attention. Two cars came pelting out of one side of the square at a crazy speed; it seemed like a hot chase. The first car was flying along and the second one was on the point of catching up with it. Suddenly the one in front braked suddenly and skidded to a halt. on the surface, and then the other car crashed into it with a loud, reverberating crash. Both cars rolled over. There was an explosion, and they caught fire. Cries and groans echoed in the falling rain, but no one hurried towards the accident. The thief carried on making his speech, and nobody paid the slightest attention to the wreckage of the two cars which was burning just a few metres away from them. They cared no more about it than they did about the rain itself. The people under the shelter noticed one of the crash victims who was crawling slowly from underneath one of the cars, splattered with blood. He tried to lift himself up on to all-fours, but fell back on to his face for the last time.

"That was a real tragedy without the slightest doubt."

"The policeman doesn't want to move!"

"There must be a telephone nearby...." But no one under the shelter moved from his place for fear of getting wet in the rain. It was coming down in torrents, and thunder was rumbling. The thief finished his speech and stood there looking self-confidently at his audience. All of a sudden, he started taking his clothes off until he stood there completely naked. He threw his clothes on top of the car wreckage now that the rain had put out the fire. He turned around as though he were showing off his naked body, and then moved two steps forwards and two steps back, dancing with a professional grace. The people who had been chasing after him started to clap in rhythm, and the boys linked arms and began to spin around them all in a continuous circle. This amazed the people under the shelter, but, in spite of everything, they held their breath.

"If it's a scene from a film, then everyone's gone mad!"

"It's a film scene, there's no doubt about it. The policeman is one of the actors waiting to play his part."

"What about the car crash?"

"That was a clever piece of artistry. Eventually, we'll discover the film director behind one of these windows...."

Just at that moment one of the windows in the building opposite the bus stop opened; the noise attracted their attention. In spite of all the clapping and the falling rain, people looked up. A fully-dressed man appeared in the window and gave a disjointed whistle. Immediately, another window in the same building opened, and a woman fully-dressed and made up appeared. She answered the whistle with a gesture of her head. They both disappeared from view and soon afterwards came out of the building together. They began walking arm in arm in the rain without seeming to care, and stopped by the two smashed cars. After exchanging some words, they began to undress until they were both completely naked in the rain. The woman lay down on the ground and put her head on top of the corpse of the man who was lying face down in the road. The man knelt down beside her. The love scene began with the movement of their arms and the touch of their lips, and then he got on top of her, covered her with his body and began making love. The dancing, clapping, the boys spinning round in a circle, the rain falling, everything continued.

"What a scandal!"

"If this is a film, then it's disgraceful. If it's really happening, then it's crazy."

"The policeman's lighting a cigarette...."

The half-empty street suddenly took on a new life.

From the South, a caravan of camels arrived with a camel driver at the front. The animals were being led by Bedouin men and women. They all set up camp a short distance away from the dancing thief's circle. The camels were all tied to the walls of the houses, and tents were put up. Then they dispersed; some started eating their food, sipping tea, or smoking, while others got involved in conversation. From the North came a group of cars full of foreign tourists. They stopped behind the thief's circle, and the passengers – men and women – got out and split up into groups. They started exploring the place avidly without paying the slightest attention to the dancing, the couple making love, the dead people in the road, or the rain.

Now lots of construction workers arrived followed by trucks loaded with stones, cement and building tools. They constructed a superb grave at an incredible speed, and made a large bed out of the stones. They covered it with sheets and decorated the supports with roses -- all this in the pouring rain. Then they went over to the wreckage of the two cars and extricated the corpses; the faces were badly smashed and the limbs were completely burned. To these they added the corpse of the man who was lying on his face in the road; he was still there underneath the man and woman and they carried on making love. The workers piled up the bodies on the bed side by side, and then turned to the two lovers. They picked them up together, but the two of them carried on copulating and made no attempt to separate. The men put them both into the grave and them covered up the entrance and poured earth over it till the whole thing was level with the ground. Then they all boarded the trucks and tore away shouting something which no one could make out.

"It's as though we're dreaming!"

"And a terrifying dream it is. The best thing woud be for us to leave...."

"No. We should wait."

"What for?"

"The happy ending."

"Happy?"

"If not, then you can tell the director it's a disaster!"

While this conversation was going on, a man wearing judge's robes sat down cross-legged on the grave. No one had noticed where he had come from; the foreign tourists, the Bedouin, the circle of dancing people, no one had any idea. He laid out a sheet of paper in front of him and started reading out a text as though he were passing sentence. No one could make out a single word he was saying since his voice was drowned by the clapping, the hubbub of people speaking in a variety of languages, and the rain. But these words of his which no one could hear were not lost. People started fighting each other in the street like roaring waves clashing violently against each other. Fights broke out around the Bedouin area, and there were yet more among the foreigners. The Bedouin started fighting the foreigners. Other people started dancing and singing. Crowds of them moved toward the grave and started making love in the nude. The thief went into ecstasy and began to dance with consummate perfection. Everything intensified and reached a climax; killing, dancing, love, death, thunder, and rain. A huge man slipped in among them. He had nothing on his head, but was wearing trousers and a black pullover and carried a magnifying-glass in his hand. He pushed his way through them roughly and with disdain, and started looking at the street with his magnifying-glass, turning around and looking at different corners as he did so.

"Not bad...not bad at all...." he muttered. The people who were huddled together under the shelter looked at him with interest.

"Him?"

"Yes...he's the director...."

The man addressed the street in a mutter again. "Carry on," he said, "No mistakes, or else we'll have to redo the whole thing from the beginning."......"

At that, one of them asked him, "Are you.... He cut him off with an aggressive and peremptory gesture. The man swallowed the rest of his question and said no more, but the nervous tension led someone else to pluck up enough courage. "Are you the director?" he asked.

The man did not pay any attention to his question but continued to look around him. Suddenly a human head rolled towards the bus-stop and came to a halt a few feet away with blood gushing in spurts from the severed neck. The men screamed in horror, but this particular man stared at the head for a moment. "Bravo...bravo...." he muttered.

"But it's a real head and real blood...." someone yelled at him.

He looked towards a man and woman who were making love. "Change the position...." he yelled impatiently, "or else you'll get bored...."

"But it was a real head," someone else shouted. "Please tell us what's going on."

"One word from you," another person said, "will be enough to tell us who you are and who these other people are...."

"There's nothing to stop you telling us!" a third person

pleaded.

But he leapt back suddenly as if to conceal himself behind them. His arrogance melted away in a look of anticipation, and the conceit in him vanished as though he had aged suddenly, or an illness which he had had suddenly become worse. The people huddled under the bus-shelter saw a group of official-looking men wandering around not far from the bus-stop like dogs smelling around. The man began to run in the rain like a maniac, and one of the people wandering around spotted him and started running after him. Others followed behind like a hurricane. Soon they were all out of sight and left the street free for the killing, loving, dancing, and the rain.

"Good heavens! He wasn't the director after all...."

"Then who was he?"

"Perhaps he was a thief...."

"Or some lunatic on the run!"

"Maybe he and the people who are chasing after him were part of a scene from the film...."

"But those things really happened. They have nothing to do with acting in a film."

"But to say that they were performing in a film is the only suggestion which makes their actions at all comprehensible."

"There's no need to start devising theories...."

"Then what's your explanation?"

"They're real, regardless of...."

"How can they possibly be real?"

"They're real."

"We must leave immediately."

"We'll be called to testify at the inquest...."

"Then there's some hope left...."

After saying that, he turned towards the policeman. "Sergeant!" he yelled.

He yelled three or four times till the policeman looked in his direction. The policeman cleared his throat and frowned. The man gestured at him to come over. "Please,

Sergeant...." he shouted.

The policeman looked at the rain with displeasure, then wrapped his cape around himself and came hurrying over to them. When he reached the shelter, he glared at them.

"What's the matter with you?" he asked.

"Didn't you see what happened in the street?" He stared fixedly at them. "Everyone standing here at the bus-stop got on their bus except for you people," he said. "What are you up to?"

"Look at this human head!"

"Where are your identification cards?" With a bitter, sarcastic smile on his face he started asking them for identification. "What's behind your meeting here?" he asked.

They all exchanged looks of innocent denial. "We don't even know each other!" one of them said.

"That's a lie, and it won't work any longer...." He stepped back two paces, aimed his rifle at them, and fired quickly and accurately. They fell down, one after another, lifeless corpses. The bodies lay there in a heap under the bus-shelter with the heads resting on the pavement in the rain.

Sleep

The solitary palm tree in the dusty courtyard was reminiscent of a cemetery. This same thought went through his mind every time he crossed the yard on his way to the outside door of the house. The landlord who was watering the ground with a hose stood in his way. "Professor!" he shouted.

Damn! This was the kind of day he hated the most, one when he had to see the landlord's face first thing in the morning. He had a soft, aged face which sometimes would break into a smile like a crack in the bark of a tree.

"You're a single man," the landlord said, "you're refined and have a good reputation. I've got no complaints against you. But what in heaven's name is the meaning of these seances you're holding in your apartment to invoke spirits?!"

"Am I to be questioned about what goes on in my apartment?"

"Yes, if the neighbors complain about it. In any case, by virtue of my long-standing friendship with your late father, I have the right to talk to you...."

Signs of anger were written all over his face.

"I've never seen you once at the Friday prayers!" the landlord continued.

"What has that got to do with the present topic?"

"Believers have no interest in such games. That's what I mean!"

The young man gave a short laugh. "But if you're interested in it," he said, "it means you believe in spirits."

"No, no! Above all else it implies doubt."

"Can I remind you about the bathroom wall?" he asked

changing the subject.

"Stop dodging the issue. The fact is that these seances are causing the people who live here a good deal of anxiety, and that is most undesirable...."

"I'm not breaking the law. I hope the wall...."

"It would be much better if we could stick to an agreement." He aimed the hose into the distance and added, "And any repairs you must get done yourself."

He really loathed seeing the landlord's face first thing in the morning on his day off. The street was almost empty as is usual in the early morning at week-ends. A stationary cloud ceiling stretched out over the neighborhood. After a night in which he had only had two hours' sleep, his head felt very heavy.

"Now's a good time to talk about Fate...." his colleague, the history teacher, had said when the seance group had broken up.

The night had come to an end without their gaining any benefit from the discussion. As he was leaving the apartment just before dawn, a friend had jokingly suggested to him that the best solution was for him to get married.

He went to bed feeling worried, and a beloved face loomed before his eyes. The palm tree did not have to stay alone forever. Why did his mother keep on assuring him a few days before her death that God should be praised for everything?!

He found the Casino empty at this early hour, and took a seat at the entrance to the garden separating the Casino from the train station. The waiter greeted him and brought him the newspapers. He made him a *ful* sandwich. When he had had enough, his head began to feel heavier and heavier. He began to wonder why he had not been able to go to sleep on his own bed when he had tried to do so. He remembered the lesson on the absolute accusative which he would be giving his students next morning, and thought of his colleague the history teacher who was his companion in their inane discussions.

"But what does that mean?"

"You're a teacher of Arabic. Fine. Can you identify a verb without a subject...?"

"Language is a boundless sea."

"Muhammad died. Muhammed is the subject, but what kind of subject is that?! Did he choose to die? That's why I'm looking for what I want outside the realm of language...."

The waiter came up to clean the marble top of the table.

"How can you justify asking the customers to pay for what they order?"

The waiter smiled as though he were used to hearing strange questions like this. He took the money and went. He told himself that the waiter was smiling like someone with intelligence. He is like me and everyone else, he thought; unless we know the absolute, then our knowledge of paltry, immediate things remain incomplete and unjustified. He stared up at the clouds till everything looked white. However, it did not stay like that for long. Some magic hand seemed to be playing with it as it melted and undulated. It changed into a dark color without any personality or shape. The train which was standing in the station disappeared or else melted away into the clouds. Spurred on by his desire for absolute peace, he was standing in front of a Buddha in the Japanese garden. He heard his friend the history teacher say as he pointed at the Buddha: 'Peace, truth, and victory'. To underline what he had said, he moved from the ideal level to reality. So he repeated it: 'Peace, truth, and defeat'. The teacher tried hard to concentrate on the discussion, but the leaves on the trees were shaken by a piercing scream; a child or maybe a woman. His heart jumped and felt aroused by a spirit of love. He wanted to quote a line from Umar al-Khayyam, but could not remember it. He tried in vain, but then a voice shouted at him. He looked round where it came from, and saw his other friend who had surprised him by saying, "The best solution is for you to get married." The sound of running feet surrounded him on all sides. He ran to catch the train, but his foot slipped and he fell down on the sidewalk. Good Lord! Where have all these people come from? Hundreds and hundreds of them standing just outside the wall of the small garden. A force of police was standing guard on the station sidewalk. Had something happened under the sluggish clouds? Here was the waiter returning to the Casino from among the crowd. He leaned over towards him. "You saw the whole thing, of course?"

He frowned in a way which registered denial and curiosity at the same time.

"You'll be called over to speak to the investigator immediately!" the waiter continued.

"What investigator?"

"The crime was committed in the station a few metres from where you're sitting."

"A crime?!" he asked in amazement.

"Where were you, Sir? A terrible murder. Don't you know the foreign girl?"

"The foreign girl!"

"An insane young man murdered her – may God take His vengeance on him!"

He screwed up his face in an agonized stupor. "Murdered," he muttered. "I don't believe it...where is she?"

"They took her to the hospital, but she died on the way."

"She died!"

"Didn't you see her when she was murdered just a few metres away?"

There were a few moments of silence. "How could you not have seen her?" the waiter continued. "I was busy inside, but, when we all heard the scream, we came running out. The wretch was chasing her and she kept running away from him, but eventually he stabbed her at the very spot where the investigator is standing now...."

"What about the murderer?"

"He was able to get away, so far at least. A small young man. The station supervisor saw him leaping over the wall and getting on a motorbike. He'll be arrested sooner or later...."

He screwed up his face even more in pain and then collapsed into his chair. The waiter left him, asking how he could possibly not have seen something which had happened right in front of him!

A policeman came up and called him over to meet the investigator. He decided to try to focus his scattered thoughts, however hard it might be. He looked at his watch, and realized that he had been asleep for an hour at least. He went over with the policeman, dragging his feet as he walked. The questions began with name, age and profession. "At what time did you come and sit down in the Casino?"

"At approximately seven in the morning."

"And you didn't leave your seat the whole time?"

"No."

"Tell us in detail, please, what you saw."

"I didn't see a thing!"

"How come? The crime was committed on this very spot. How come you didn't see anything?"

"I was asleep!"

"Asleep!"

"Yes," he replied in shame.

"Didn't the noise of the chase wake you up?"

"No."

"Nor the screams?"

He shook his head, biting his lip.

"Didn't you hear her calling for help, when she called you by name?"

"She called my name?!" he yelled with a moan.

"Yes, she yelled at you several times, and the witnesses presumed she was running towards you to ask for help!"

He stared at the investigator in amazement. "No!" he muttered pleadingly.

"That's exactly what happened."

He closed his eyes, and paid no more attention to the investigator or his questions. Eventually the latter got very angry. "Answer the questions," he said, "you are obliged to answer...."

"I feel utterly miserable...."

"Was there any relationship between you and her?"

"No...."

"But she called you by name?"

"We were from the same neighborhood and lived in neighboring streets...."

"Witnesses have testified that they have often seen you both standing next to each other waiting for the train...."

"Just because we happened to go to work at the same time...."

"Doesn't the fact that she asked you for help mean something?"

"Perhaps she was aware of the fact that I liked her!"

"Then there was some kind of relationship between you."

"Perhaps...." he said. "I loved her," he continued with great emotion. "I often used to think about asking for her hand."

"Didn't you do anything about it?"

"No...I hadn't made up my mind yet."

"You say you were asleep when it happened?"

He lowered his head with an excruciating feeling of shame.

"The other man, the murderer,...have you got any ideas about who he might be?"

"No."

"You've never heard of her having an affair with anyone else?"

"No."

"Didn't you ever see anyone lurking around her?"

"No."

"Have you anything else to add?"

"No."

The sky was still hidden behind the solid cloud ceiling. Some drizzle fell for a minute, then it stopped. He wandered around aimlessly for a long time.

The day came to an end with him still wandering around as though he were trying to cure the pain of this agonizing disaster though physical exertion. The history teacher ran into him in front of the Japanese garden and shook his hand. "Come on," he said, "let's sit down together. I want to talk."

"I'm sorry, but I have no desire to talk metaphysics."

His friend's mouth tightened in disappointment. "Is what they're saying true?" he asked. "Was the foreign girl murdered right in front of you while you were asleep?"

"Who told you that?" he asked angrily.

"I heard about it at the barber's." he replied apologetically.

"Is it so incredible for a tired man to feel sleepy...? How can you blame him if the heavens fall in while he's

His friend laughed. "Don't get angry," he said in a friendly tone. "I didn't realize that there was anything between you and the foreign girl."

"What do you mean?...you're crazy...."

"Excuse me...excuse me...that's what I heard them saying at the barber's shop...."

He went on his way aimlessly. Damn it. The rumors would start spreading like wildfire. No power on earth could bring that beautiful, luscious girl back to life. An incurable feeling of grief swept over him. Her despairing cries for help had crashed against his wall of sleep in vain, but they had reached the ears of the neighborhood through some magic means. You poor girl, I'm even more wretched than you are.

"You have my sympathy, Sir," the cigarette seller said to him as he handed him the packet of cigarettes. "I'm very sorry to hear about her death...."

Damn it! There does not seem to be anyone who has not heard about what happehed. Here they all are offering him their complete condolences. They are all convinced there was something between them. And now, the eulogy being spoken after someone has died. Perhaps people's thoughts are stretching even beyond that.

The grocer gave him a meaningful look. What about the grocer anyway?! Even so, it seemed to him that everyone's eyes were following him. Actually, he was being pursued; accused, a criminal. He was responsible for answering the lost cries for help. There was no escape. Tomorrow in school, questions would hail down on him, but the real hell with its raging flames would come in the school courtyard. He wandered around for a long time, hearing a number of things all of which were irksome and painful to him. He was the subject of the neighborhood gossip; all they could talk about was the crime and the fact that he had been asleep.

"They've arrested the murderer; he's a secondary boy."

So it was the absurd and the young kid's madness which had caused her death.

"The murderer loved her, but she didn't encourage him at all."

So that is why she always seemed so grave and serious to him.

"It's quite certain now that she was in love with the Arabic teacher."

What a shame.... Instead of being concerned about making her happy, he had spent his time on spiritual seances, and sleep had prevented him from rescuing her.

"During the inquest, he said he was asleep. Isn't it funny that the screams, the sound of the chase, and the cries for help didn't wake him up?"

It really was incredible, but they did not realize that he had spent the previous night at a seance and talking about fate. Pain had a strong hold on his heart, and he swallowed it like a slow poison. In the end, he had to return to the house, albeit unwillingly. The rain water was covering the veil of clouds with a dark shroud. He found the owner sitting on a bench under the solitary palm tree. The latter welcomed him cordially. "You look tired," he said. "I hope my conversation with you this morning didn't annoy you?"

"Is what they're saying true?" the owner asked him lowering his voice.

"Yes," he replied, interrupting angrily. "The foreign girl was murdered a few metres from my seat in the Casino while I was asleep. It's the eighth wonder of the world!"

"My dear boy, I didn't mean...."

"I didn't hear her cries for help," he said, interrupting again. "Other people claim I did hear, but just pretended to be asleep...."

The man came up to him apologizing profusely. He took him by the arm and sat him down beside him. "Your late father was my friend," he said. "Don't blame me, my son...."

A substantial time went by in circumspect silence. Then he asked to be excused, and the old man escorted him to the inside door: "I beg you once again," he whispered in his ear. "to bear in mind what I told you about those seances!"

He threw himself on his bed. The strain was dreadful. He closed his eyes. "I need a long sleep," he muttered, " a long, endless sleep...."

The Heart Doctor's Ghost

The man examined her with interest. She met his gaze with cautious inquiring eyes. He was sitting with his back against the door of the small tomb, while she sat cross-legged in front of him. They were the only two people in the desolate square in front of the tomb, in the company of the early morning rays of sunshine. The tomb itself was small, like a prison cell. There seemed to be no proportion between the man's thin body, his big green turban and his thick black beard. There was an even more striking contrast between the girl's dress which was ragged and dirty, her bare feet, and the captivating beauty of her face. The man pointed to the tomb. "Bless his memory," he said. "He did marvellous things in surgery."

"Bless his memory," she muttered naively.

"Could it be that you have come to see him because of some wound which man cannot cure?"

"Yes," she murmured in a somewhat simple-minded fashion.

"How old are you, girl?" he asked her suspiciously.

"I don't know."

"But surely your mother knows?"

"I never had a mother...."

"Is she dead?"

"I don't know."

"Where's your father?"

"I never had a father."

"Where do you live?"

"In the world!"

"What's your job?"

"I sell rotten fruit which the fruit seller either gives me or sells very cheaply."

"But that's a rotten trade!"

"There are some customers who will fight to get a bit of it."

"Where do you live?"

"In the wilderness during summer, and under the arcades in winter."

"Can you stand the changes in weather?"

"Do they do any harm?!"

The man lowered his voice somewhat. "Have you kept your honour intact, girl?" he asked her.

"My honour?!"

He paused for a moment. "Hasn't a young man ever seduced you?" he asked.

"Seduced me?!"

"Deceived you so as to have his way with you?"

"We work together, play together, and sleep together!"

"Curse it!"

"Curse it?!"

"Could it be you came to see the saint in the tomb because you feel you are being chased by your own guilty conscience?"

"Conscience?!"

"Don't you know what conscience is either!?"

"Either?"

"Are you happy with your life?"

"Life is beautiful," she replied enthusiastically, "in spite of there being numerous conflicts."

"So it's conflicts which are worrying you?"

"No! They give life its sweet taste!"

"What is your religion, girl?" the man asked, breathing out as he did.

"My religion?!"

"Don't you know what religion is?"

"Religion?"

"What brought you to see me?" he asked her angrily.

"It was you who told me to sit down, so I sat."

"But I saw you coming towards me, didn't I?"

"Towards the tomb!"

"Why?"

"I thought it would be a good shelter for me."

"Are you naive or insane?"

The girl resorted to silence.

"You live in the wilderness in summer and under the arcades in winter," he said, "so what made you look for shelter?"

She seemed to be on the point of replying, but closed her lips and remained silent.

"You're a devil!" the man muttered angrily.

"Who are you?" she asked simply.

"Only devils don't know who I am," he replied in anger.

"What is your job?"

"You don't know the meaning of honour or religion, so how can you know the meaning of sainthood?"

"Why are you angry?"

"Accursed you will be in both worlds!"*

"Both worlds?"

"In this world and in the hereafter...."

"I know this world, but what's the hereafter?"

"Get out of my sight!"

The girl stood up. A piece of jewelry fell from inside her dress and landed at her feet. She stooped quickly and picked it up, but the saint's hand clasped her arm firmly. He leapt to his feet. "What's this?" he asked.

She yelled at him to let go of her arm, but he grabbed hold of her shoulders and started shaking her roughly. Pieces of jewelry began falling out till there was a little treasure trove lying on the ground.

At that moment, the warden of the tomb appeared. He saw the man and the girl struggling, and then noticed the treasure. His eyes moved from one to the other, and then

* The language is very formal in the original at this point.

came to a stop, staring at the jewels in bewilderment. "What's going on?" he asked.

"She's one of those street scavengers," the saint replied.

"What brought her here?"

"The devil thought she could hide her loot in the tomb."

"What do you intend to do with her?"

"What must be done."

"Leave me alone," the girl wailed.

"Shut up, you thief," the man yelled at her.

"You're crushing my bones."

"Where did you get this jewelry from?"

"It belongs to me!"

"Did you inherit it from your family?"

"What are you going to do with her?" the warden of the tomb asked again.

"What must be done." the saint replied.

"And what's that?"

"We must hand her over to the police."

"Isn't it possible that she's innocent?"

"Justice will bring out the complete truth."

"But justice is blind, my dear saint."

"How did she get these jewels?"

"God gives to those whom He wishes without calculation."

"Do you think we should let her go?"

"She won't be safe from highway robbers."

"It only remains then for me to take her into my care!"

"But you're a saint. How can you possibly look after worldly matters?"

"What weird dreams you keep having!" the saint commented suspiciously.

"Perhaps they're the same ones you are having!"

The girl interrupted, pleading with them to let her go. The saint loosened his grip on her arm. "It's not safe for you in the world of wickedness," he said.

"I'll open up the tomb just as you want!" the warden

told her.

"I want to go!" the girl yelled insistently. She tried to free her arm, but the saint tightened his grip. The warden of the tomb came up to help him. They exchanged glances over the girl's head.

"We need time to discuss things," the warden said. They exchanged a wink and then carried the girl backwards inside the tomb. They were inside for a few minutes, and then emerged dripping with perspiration. The warden locked the door of the tomb, then came over to the saint. "It will be better if we come to some sort of agreement," he said.

"Don't forget, she came up to me of her own accord."

"No, she was making for the tomb."

"Tell me what you have in mind."

"Let's split the loot!"

"It would be more just to...."

But the warden of the tomb interrupted firmly, "Let's split the loot!"

The saint was silent for a while. "What shall we do with the girl?" he asked.

"Let's drive her away and threaten her with all kinds of trouble if she comes back."

"Maybe...."

"She's a thief. She won't go running to the police."

"She may come back with a gang of thugs whom we won't be able to fight."

"Do you think it would be better to get rid of her?"

"What do you mean?"

"Kill her!"

"Kill her?!"

"Then bury her in the tomb; it's empty, as you know."

"But I haven't got the heart to kill anybody!" said the saint anxiously.

"Nor have I...." replied the warden in relief.

"What shall we do then?"

They both remained silent, deep in thought. Then the warden of the tomb said triumphantly, " I think we should ask our friend the policeman for help!"

"Good idea!...."

"It's the only way out we have."

"But the loot will have to be split three ways instead of two!"

"That's better than losing it all." The warden went away and was gone for a long time. Then he came back with the policeman.

"That's the problem, no more and no less." he was telling him.

The policeman shook his head as he was thinking. The saint came towards him. "The decision is yours to make," he said, "and then you must carry it out."

"But it's a problem which needs to be solved," the policeman said, "one which is fraught with risks!"

"You arrest the girl," the saint suggested, "and start your investigation of her immediately. Then you take possession of the jewelry in the name of the law. At that point, we will intercede on her behalf to have her released. As soon as you release your hold on her, she will fly away like a dove and will never come back to this place as long as she lives!"

"But I cannot accept any injustice...." the policeman replied.

"What injustice!" the warden cried in bewilderment. "She's a wicked thief, a highway-robber!"

"The injustice," the policeman replied, "is that the loot should be divided equally among us!"

The two men were stunned.

"If it wasn't for our close friendship with you," the saint said, "we'd have done the job ourselves."

"You wouldn't have resorted to asking me if it hadn't been necessary!"

"My dear friend, don't misjudge us."

"Half for me and a quarter for each of you."

"Don't go too far, my friend."

"Don't waste time in vain...." He was silent for a while. "But we'll need an appraiser," he continued.

"An appraiser!?"

"For weighing, valuing, and examining the jewels."

"Do you think he would do it for nothing?"*

"What have you ever done for nothing?"

"But that will give each of us a smaller share, won't it?"

"Both of you, yes!!"

"We must carry the new burden equally."

"You seem to forget you're addressing the law!"

"My dear friend, have some mercy!"

"The law doesn't shut its eyes without a price."

"I'm the owner of what's been found," the saint said.

"I'm in charge of the tomb," the warden said.

"Is there any greater mercy than giving you riches instead of dragging you off to prison?!" the policeman retorted angrily.

A stunned silence fell on both of them, made even heavier by their surrender. The policeman took the jewels, and suggested that he take them to the appraiser, but the two men insisted on accompanying him. As they were on the point of leaving, a blind old man came up holding the arm of a blind young man; he was heading in the direction of the tomb. The three men postponed their departure, just to reassure themselves. The old man reached the door of the tomb, and stretched out his hand towards it.

"Where is the warden of the tomb?" he asked in a loud voice.

"It seems he's ill," the policeman answered. "Go away and come back tomorrow."

"A locked door will never block the path of mercy," the old man said. "The Merciful one so ordered."

He leaned the young man's head on the door. "Doctor of broken hearts!" he shouted. "I bring you my poor son. He has lost his sight in an accident, and all his efforts at earning a living have come to nothing. The doctors have failed to cure him. Give him the fullness of your blessing...."

* Lit. "for God's sake, for charity"

The three men were about to move off again when the blind young man let out a yell, "Lord in heaven above!"

"What's the matter, my son?" the old man asked.

"I heard a voice!"

"What voice, my son?"

"The voice of the doctor of broken hearts and no other!" The three men exchanged glances in panic. The old man put his ear to the door. "What did you hear, my son?" he asked.

"His voice went straight to the depths of my heart...."

"Go away and come back tomorrow," the policeman told them angrily.

"I won't go," the young man shouted. "He's calling me!"

"I'm a policeman," the policeman said. "I'm telling you, I can't hear anything...."

"Quiet!" the young man yelled at the top of his voice. "Let the voice of mercy penetrate to my heart...."

"But you are breaking the law!"

"Shut up! The heart doctor is whispering in my ear. Speak, doctor of broken hearts!"

The blind young man's voice seemed to attract the attention of some people, and they began flocking barefoot to the courtyard with their blue *gallabiyyas*. They stood there watching with interest and exchanging whispers. The three men felt that some unknown danger was imminent. The saint and the warden of the tomb urged the policeman to save the situation before things got out of control. The policeman stamped the ground with his foot.

"Young man, stop that babbling," he yelled in a rough and commanding tone.

But the young man yelled loudly, "The heart doctor is calling me."

"Stop that babbling...."

"Have pity on his youth and infirmity," the old man implored.

"He's causing a disturbance."

"Let him hear whatever comes to his ears," the old man said. "There's no harm in that for anyone."

More than one voice from among the bystanders said, "There's no harm in that for anyone, there's no harm in that for anyone." The young man continued to address the tomb.

"Heart doctor," he said, "I hear you. Your voice fills my heart, it stirs the very depths of my soul. I am climbing on the road to heaven, heart doctor...." Some people shouted, "Blessed be God the All-powerful."

"This is delusion," the policeman yelled. "This is a defiance of the security laws."

"Go to some saint of God or a state doctor!" said the saint.

"The age of miracles is over!" said the warden of the tomb.

"Blessed be God the All-powerful," some people repeated.

The young man carried on with his conversation. "Heart doctor," he said. "How beautiful your voice is; gentle as mercy, whispering like a secret, precious as light...."

"Utter humbug!" the policeman yelled. "You're convening a public gathering without permission from the Ministry of the Interior!"

But the young man carried on talking. "I'm listening to you with my entire being; I'm listening, bringer of light and hope."

The policeman stepped forward a few paces towards the crowd. "In the name of the law," he yelled, "I order you to disperse." More than one voice said, "Let us see a miracle...."

"Go away. If you don't, I'll use a stick and force you to leave!"

"No power will ever stop us seeing a blessed miracle."

The policeman leapt to his feet to attack them, and the crowd leapt up to defend themselves without moving from the places where they were standing. Suddenly the blind young man let out a yell. "Open the door, open the door," he cried. "This is the heart doctor's command...."

The people started raising a hue and cry. "Open the door, open the door...." several of them yelled.

"He's calling me!" the blind young man shouted pleadingly.

"Open the door," voices yelled out in a crazy fervour. "The ghost wants to be let out...."

"I will not open it," the warden of the tomb said, "in deference to security and the law...."

Whereupon, the young man started pushing the door with his shoulder. The crowd started yelling. The policeman tried to stop him by using force, but the young man drove him away roughly and pushed him out of the way. The crowd started yelling and the three men were forced to move to one side, yielding in the face of their anger.

The door opened under the weight of the young man's powerful pushing, and shouts filled the courtyard like an explosion. The young man did not hesitate, but went into the tomb, feeling his way with his hands until he was out of sight. Outside, there was total and profound silence; people used their inquiring eyes as a focus to express their inner feelings. Time and Place meant nothing.

Suddenly, a shout was heard from inside, and the young man appeared at the door of the tomb stumbling as he walked. He looked up at the sky. "I call God to witness," he shouted, "I can see! I call God to witness, my sight has come back!" He looked around at the faces of the stunned and silent people. "I can see light," he yelled, "I can see people, I can see the sky, and I've seen the ghost!"

"The ghost!"

"It appeared to me in the form of a girl bound in chains...."

"God is most great...God is most great."

"It was God's will that I break her chains!"

"God is most great...God is most great."

"She radiated an aura of splendour, majesty and beauty...."

"God is most great...God is most great."

"God willing, she'll appear to the eyes of the faithful!"

The young man rushed towards the crowd and stood in front of them facing the door of the tomb. Silence prevailed yet again, and everyone looked towards the door in an agony of anticipation. The girl appeared with slow, hesitant steps, and looked at the crowd in bewilderment. A cry rose up from the depths and everyone prostrated themselves in humility.

"God is most great...."

"God is All-powerful."

"How beautiful it is."

"How radiant it is."

"No one has ever seen the like of it before...." Some people turned towards the three men who were still standing and yelled at them to prostrate themselves. They were forced to do so in response to the furious command.

"I'm your servant from now and forever...." the young man shouted.

The crowd vied with each other to show their humility.

"Look after those who are absent."

"Mercy on the sick."

"Be gracious to the poor labourer."

"Bring down your wrath on the unjust."

The girl looked at what was going on around her in amazement. "Where am I?" she asked.

"You've come down from the heavens to our wretched earth...." the young man replied.

"What am I seeing?"

"People brought together by a miracle after they had been scattered by anxieties."

"I feel dizzy."

"That's the dizziness which someone feels when they bewail the situation we are in."

"They almost suffocated me!"

"A curse on the culprits whoever they were and where-ever they are now."

"They stole the jewelry without mercy...."

"Your gems* are for good people, not pilferers."

"I want the jewels...."

"May everyone who believes in you dedicate his precious gems to you!"

The three men saw that the crowd was preoccupied with the girl, and took the opportunity to start backing away so that they could escape. But the girl's eyes fell on the saint and the warden of the tomb.

"There are the two criminals," she yelled, pointing at them.

Some men pounced on the two of them and pushed them forward till they fell to the ground in front of the girl. "Where are the jewels?" she asked them.

The two men resorted to silence.

"The blessed ghost is talking about real jewels!" said a man in the crowd.

"The ghost speaks in a language which no human can comprehend!" the policeman commented.

"She's speaking about real jewels."

"Beware of interpreting the ghost's words to suit your own desires," the policeman repeated.

"Beat the two of them until they confess!"

"I'm responsible for public security."

"Beat them till they confess!"

"We're God's folk," the saint said in alarm.

"Search us if you wish," said the warden of the tomb.

"Beat them till they confess!" some men in the crowd yelled.

The two men were then set upon with a hail of blows

---

* The Arabic word here (jauhar) has the double meaning of 'jewel' and 'essence'. The word 'gem' is used here to convey the figurative meaning, since Mahfuz is implying both senses of the word in this passage.

till the warden of the tomb gave in. "The policeman has taken charge of the jewels," he yelled.

The enraged crowd turned towards the policeman. He stood up and spoke to them in rapid, panic-stricken phrases. "I arrested them while they were dividing up the jewels," he said. "I took possession of them in the name of the law...."

The policeman got rid of the jewels without hesitation, and put them down on the courtyard floor in front of the tomb to the accompaniment of a surging wave of *takbirs** and *tahlils **.

"Now the truth is coming to light!" the young man shouted.

Gradually the voices died down till there was silence, then the young man resumed. "The ghost wanted to give some jewels to the poor," he said, "and these two robbers stole them from her; but now they have been returned to their owners!"

"God is most great...God is most great."

"That is the heart doctor's mission to you...."

"God bless you, heart doctor."

"Let the jewels be divided up equally."

"God bless you, heart doctor!"

"And let them be spent on good works."

"God bless you, heart doctor!"

Suddenly a respectable-looking young man came hurrying up and looked at what was going on around him in bewilderment. Then his eyes fell on the jewels, and he rushed towards them like a madman. "My stolen jewels," he yelled.

The young man pushed him away so hard that he reeled backwards. "They're my jewels," the man yelled. "Their description and weight are all noted down in the police

* The act of saying *Allahu Akbar* (God is most great).
** The act of saying *La-llah illa l-lah* (There is no God but God).

record...."

"You liar!" said voices coming from the crowd.

"Thief!"

"You're an accomplice of the two criminals."

"Let's go to the police station," the man said.

"Go to hell."

As he was being set on, his eyes fell on the girl. He look-ed at her in astonishment. "You!" he yelled. He was about to pounce on her, but the young man gave him a hard push which almost knocked him to the ground.

"Speak politely, you rogue...." the crowd yelled at him in a fury.

"You don't deserve to stand in front of a gracious ghost."

"What has happened to the world?!" the man asked himself in bewilderment. He noticed the policeman and went over to ask him for help.

"The jewelry's mine," he said. "Take us to the station...."

"Be patient," the policeman whispered in his ear. "There's no point in aggravating the crowd now."

"But she's a thief, a crook!"

A hail of fists rained down on him.

"Cut your tongue out, you wretch!"

"Windbag!"

"Vile wretch."

"What have you to say about this wretch?" the young man asked the girl.

"He's an animal," she answered quickly, "who wallows in the dust of young girls and then is niggardly about giving them any *milliemes!*"

"Animal...animal," the crowd yelled in fury.

"You can take his money," the girl said. "I hereby make it lawful for you!"

Takbirs and *tahlils* arose. Strong men set about him and knocked him to the ground. Then they took all his money out of his pockets.

"Policeman!" the respectable-looking man yelled.

"What can the police do among lunatics!" muttered the policeman.

"I'm being robbed of my money in your presence!"

"His money is the heart doctor's gift to the poor just like the jewels!" yelled the young man.

"God bless the gracious ghost!" shouted the crowd.

"Let's divide the money up equally...." the young man said.

The crowd gathered round the young man, and they began dividing up the money and the jewels. The respectable-looking man started babbling. "What's happened to the world?" he asked.

"Now the heart doctor's mission has been fulfilled," the young man said.

The girl pointed at the respectable-looking man, the policeman, the warden of the tomb and the saint. "Tie them up and lock them up in the tomb!" she said.

The crowd pounced on the four men, tied them up and then carried them inside the tomb and locked the door. The girl gave the key to the young man. "Now you're the warden of the tomb...." she said. Then she looked at the crowd. "Go now," she said, " and God be with you...." They left in spite of themselves; the only one who remained with her was the young man, the new warden of the tomb. They exchanged glances, of humility on his side, and of longing on hers.

"Why didn't you take part of the money?" she asked.

"For me," the young man replied, showing his infatuation, "it's enough to be warden of the tomb."

"What did you do before you lost your sight?"

"I was raised in the street till that kind old man took me away and taught me his trade which is making perfume essence!"

"You were a street boy?"

"That is the first thing in life I can remember."

"How did you lose your sight?"

"I was hit by a passing car!"

"But now you have it back. Congratulations...."

"Thanks to God and to you."

She thought for a moment. "The best plan would be for you to go back to your original job with the kind old man...." she said.

"But I want to stay on as warden of your tomb...."

"I'm telling you to return to your job...."

"Is that an order?"

"Yes."

"Then I'll return to my job...."

"I'll be sending you a girl who grew up there too. When you see her, you will think you are seeing me...."

"How wonderful to be able to see your image forever...."

"Marry her; I give her to you...."

"Hearing is obeying...."

"Treat her kindly."

"Hearing is obeying...."

"Don't believe what you hear from people who are jealous of her...."

"Hearing is obeying...."

"Don't leave her till death parts you from her."

"Hearing is obeying."

"Now go in peace...."

"I wanted to stay like your shadow...."

"Go in peace."

The young man bowed his head in obedience, then left looking sad and disappointed. She found herself alone in the wilderness. "What has happened to the world?" she asked herself in confusion.

"Either I'm mad or they are!" she continued with a frown.

"Everyone was prostrating themselves, and saying *takbirs* and *tahlils*. One gesture from me and they all responded...what happened?!"

Suddenly she heard the sound of someone pushing on the door of the tomb from the inside. She took to her heels in a panic. The door opened under the force of the pushing, and the respectable-looking man, the policeman, the warden of the tomb and the saint emerged. The respectable-looking man yelled at the policeman. "I hold you responsible for the entire farce," he said angrily.

"Be patient," the policeman replied, "nothing could be done. The crowd had gone mad, and when that happens, all respect for the police disappears. But don't imagine that any criminal is going to slip through my hands...."

"The crooked little thief, where has she gone?"

"You can reckon she's as good as in your grasp; I mean what I say."

"How can we get my money and jewels back?"

"Let's go to the station for help...." the warden of the tomb suggested.

"No, no!" the policeman objected. "Investigations have various byways which scare me!"

"What's to be done then?" asked the saint.

"I have my own special ways," replied the policeman.

"No," said the respectable-looking man, "I've an idea which will get back my lost jewels if it works."

"And what's that?"

"We'll ask the ghost for help!"

"The ghost?!"

"The ghost which robbed me of my jewels can help me get them back again!"

"That's just a dream."

"We'll go over the whole action of the drama again!"

"The same one?"

"But we'll provide the actors."

"Where can we find the ghost?"

"The same one. If she won't play her part, we'll tear her limb from limb!"

◆ ◆ ◆ ◆

The following morning, the first rays of the sun shone on the tomb. It was locked, and the saint was sitting by the door. Suddenly he saw an old man coming towards the tomb, leading a blind young man behind him. Men came and took up their positions near the tomb. The saint winked at them and they started shouting and pretending to be astonished about something.

"Are we really seeing another miracle?"

"Yes indeed...is it a new miracle?"

Their raised voices carried to the outskirts of the city, and the crowd of the day before came hurrying back to the square in front of the tomb with the young man at their head. The policeman and the warden of the tomb joined them, and everyone's eyes were focused on the blind young man. They saw him lean his head on the tomb door. "Lord in heaven!" he shouted.

"What's the matter my son?" the old man asked.

"I hear a voice, father," the young man replied with great excitement.

A whisper went through the crowd which rapidly changed into *tahlils* and *takbirs*. The warden of the tomb feigned alarm. "Policeman!" he yelled urgently.

"The lesson I learned yesterday is enough for me," the policeman answered submissively. "Let it be as God wills...."

The crowd yelled in victory. "He is calling me!" the blind young man shouted.

"God is most great...God is most great," the crowd shouted.

"He is calling me!"

"God is most great...God is most great," the crowd shouted.

"I am listening, doctor of broken hearts, I'm at your beck and call."

"God the All-powerful be blessed!"

"Open the door. He's calling me. Open the door...."

The young man of the previous day came up and opened the door to the accompaniment of *tahlils* and *takbirs*. The blind young man went in, feeling his way into the heart of the tomb till he was out of sight. Silence prevailed; a total, profound silence. People used their inquiring eyes as a focus to express their inner feelings. Suddenly a shout was heard from inside. The young man emerged at the door and lifted his hands to the sky. "I call God to witness," he yelled, "my sight is restored!" Everyone felt drawn into saying, "God is most great...God is most great...."

"The world has been created anew, with its light and its people. Heart doctor, may you accept me as a warden for your tomb!"

"God the All-powerful be blessed...."

"The blessing is God's. How beautiful light is after darkness...."

"God bless the gracious ghost...."

"What did you find inside?" asked one of the people standing in the front row.

"I saw the ghost tied up in chains!"

"What can have tied her up," the young man of the day before asked in amazement, "after I set her free with my own hands?"

"I have told you what I saw...."

Pleas for help followed one another in quick succcession.

"Accomplish your gracious favours for us, heart doctor."

"Reliever of adversities."

"Helper of the weak and the poor...."

The girl appeared in the doorway as she had done on the previous day, and the place echoed with *tahlils* and *takbirs*.

"Here is the blessed ghost."

"Wait and see; there will be even more blessings...."

"Blessed be the poor...."

"Where am I?" asked the girl.

Many voices competed to answer, "On the earth which you're enriching with your generosity."

"What am I seeing?"

"Your grateful people."

"The chains almost stifled me!" she said in a distressed tone of voice.

"Who was the accursed criminal?" demanded voices raised in fury.

"Who was the foul rogue?"

"Who is an enemy of ghosts?"

"A friend threw me into those chains, not an enemy," the girl said, looking despairingly at the people around her. "He had good intentions, not bad."

Their mouths gaped open in astonishment.

"The only thing which caused me harm," she continued, "was a misunderstanding and misinterpretation!"

They kept on staring at her with astonished and questioning looks.

"I threw you a riddle, and you fell into its traps!"

"God forgive us...."

"You didn't realize that ghosts don't speak in the language of the world."

"God forgive us."

"They give eternal light, not ephemeral wealth!"

"God forgive us," shouted the people in the front row. The rest of them stood there in stunned silence with their heads bowed.

"The Ghost came to purify people's hearts, not to encourage them to plunder and steal!"

The crowd succumbed to a profound silence.

"God forgive us," the rest shouted.

"That's how you fell into error and robbed people of their rightful possessions!"

"God forgive us."

"That was the thing which put me back into prison."

"God forgive us."

"Release me, my loyal friends."

To the accompaniment of *tahlils* and *takbirs*, the people in the front row began delving into their pockets and threw the money at the girl's feet. The crowd looked uneasy, and each one withdrew within himself feeling depressed and in low spirits. They started looking at each other as though they were waking up from a dream, while the others became impatient with them.

"Are you being niggardly about the gracious ghost's freedom?" the policeman remonstrated with them.

But one of them didn't say a word or move. The young man of the previous day started staring at the girl in amazement. "What am I seeing?" he yelled eventually with a groan.

Everyone looked at him.

"How tremendously everything has altered!" he yelled angrily at the girl. "What am I seeing?"

Everyone glued their eyes on him as he stared piercingly at the girl with a mad intensity.

"You're not the gracious ghost!" he shouted defiantly.

The eyes of the crowd gleamed with hope. "Stop that nonsense, you heretic!" the policeman yelled at him.

"You aren't gracious ghost!" he again shouted insistently.

The hearts of the crowd emitted a warm wave of response to what he was saying; they believed him from the bottom of their tortured souls. People's expressions changed, and in the process so did the person at whom they were looking. Angry outbursts followed one another in rapid succession:

"You're not the gracious ghost!"

"Where's that kindly voice of yesterday?"

"Where has the mercy of the heavens gone?"

"Where has that majesty and splendour disappeared?"

"Look at the tattered rags she's wearing!"

"Look at the dirt all over her feet."

"Look at the dust covering her face!"

Suddenly the girl leapt up and broke through the barrier which was surrounding her. She threw herself into the midst of the crowd shouting, "Help!"

"What's this?" the policeman yelled.

"I'm a poor girl," she shouted, "not a ghost or an angel!"

"You little cheat," the policeman yelled, "a curse on you...."

"They threatened to kill me," the girl shouted, "if I didn't say what they wanted."

Voices rose in anger and people started clenching their fists. Some of the conspirators* pounced on the girl, but the crowd stopped them. A fierce battle broke out between the two sides in which hands, feet, sticks, bricks and teeth were all in use. Each side fought stubbornly and furiously. The young man of the previous day saw the girl fighting like a man, and it occurred to him that she was his promised girl. That made him even stronger and more reckless.

◆ ◆ ◆ ◆

The battle went on, becoming increasingly vicious and brutal.

---

* i.e., people in the front row.

The Window on the Thirty–fifth Floor

He stretched out his legs and sank back into the soft armchair. The day had been full of activity, and he felt a little exhausted. The old servant put on the lights in the hall and then cast a final glance over the bar and sumptuous table. He was just about to leave.

"Put the lights out till the guests arrive," he was told.

The servant did as he was asked and then left. His master's thin frame disappeared in the invisible darkness. He began to look out through the window in the wall facing him; he could see the Muqattam Hills beyond the Nile, the fields and the eastern part of the city. "Another birthday," he told himself, "with seven symbolic candles. Many, many years, but how few friends there are left...."

He closed his eyes. "I wonder how many loaves of bread I've devoured," he muttered to himself, "how much veal and lamb, how many acres of greens and vegetables; how much Nile water I've drunk and how many calories I've used up working and playing." He had a long yawn. "It's a lucky man," he thought, "who can reach this great age with a happy conscience!"

He abandoned himself to silence to recuperate his energy. He was happy floating in a profound silence but then he heard some clothes rustle or someone breathing. He opened his eyes and saw an old man standing almost in the centre of the hall; he was wearing tattered clothes and no shoes and had only one eye.

"Who are you?" he asked the man. But then he looked more closely. "My poor old neighbor!" he said in astonishment.

The old man did not say a word.

"Unforgettable memories of younger days," he said. "How did you manage to get up to my apartment on the thirty-fifth floor?"

The old man did not answer; he did not seem to want to talk.

"Do you need something? Is that why you've come here?" He waited in vain for an answer. "Do you need some money or old clothes as you did in the past?" he asked.

The old man stepped back a few paces.

"I've thought about you several times," the man continued, "but I thought you were dead!"

The old man spoke for the first time. "You weren't wrong," he replied coldly.

"Really?"

"Really!"

"Maybe you've come to wish me a happy birthday."

"Damn you!" was the reply in a coarse voice.

"Damn me?!"

"Yes, damn you and all criminals!" The old man moved back a few paces and then disappeared completely. He had vanished before the fire which his questions had kindled had died down; before there had been any chance to find out why he was so angry with him or why he was not grateful for his kindness.

"What's going on in the next world," he asked himself, "which is proving so hard for us to take?"

Suddenly he heard a gentle voice addressing him. "Are you still talking to yourself like a lunatic?" it asked him.

There she stood in front of him wearing her billowing house coat, blooming with health and energy.

"You!!" he yelled fearfully.

"Yes, me and no one else," she replied," with all my memories."

"What painful memories they are," he said, "my heart isn't rid of them yet."

"Amazing!"

"That's why I've refused to get married and have remained a bachelor till the very end."

"But all you did was be my lover."

"Even though you were the equivalent of my mother; my father's wife...."

"Everthing is possible in the course of love and passion."

"The crime still disturbs my peace of mind."

"Do you call it a crime?"

"It was you who tempted me!"

"We both tempted each other...."

"It's the one hellish memory in my life.

"It's the happiest of my memories."

"You...."

"Good woman, just as you're a good man."

"Is that the way they look at it over there?"

"How is it you didn't hear? Happy Birthday...."

She disappeared. His mind was all confused, but even so, he felt a warm feeling of relaxation inside him. His load of worries vanished. "Who knows," he told himself, "maybe I went too far in holding myself responsible when that young man I didn't know drowned...."

He heard a deep sigh, and saw the young man standing naked in front of him and staring into his face.

"So you say you went too far, do you?" he said.

"I began to think so," he replied hopefully.

"You shameless liar!"

They stared at each other for a long while until he began to feel uneasy.

"You left me to drown, you wretch!" the young man said.

"It wasn't my fault," he replied, "you are responsible and only you."

"The waves were too strong and my strength gave out, so I called to you for help...."

"I wasn't any good at swimming...."

"Rubbish, you were good enough to save me....but you

ran away, you murderer."

"Don't say that. At that time, the law itself...."

"The law! Drowning people are the responsibility of the people who are watching!"

"I thought you would see the situation in a new light."

"Why should I?"

"That's the way laws change in your world!"

"They changed in your head because you were afraid. I'm sorry I even spoke to you...."

The young man went away and left him in a state of anxiety which made him lose his sense of reason. He no longer felt at ease, and contradictory thoughts were churning around inside his troubled mind. "What's good and what's bad?" he asked himself. "How can my conscience find its way in this jungle full of conflicting peculiarities!! If only my father were alive!"

"Thank you for your good opinion of me!" said a voice which he had not heard for a very long time.

To avoid looking at his father straight in the face, he closed his eyes. Shame made him tongue-tied, and he did not say a word.

"I see you're preparing to celebrate your birthday!" his father said in a tone of voice which had a certain amount of sarcasm to it. "What's stopping you from saying something?" he asked when his son failed to say anything.

"The guilt," he answered in a shattered voice. "It was a heavy one!"

"Can you still remember that?"

"How could I ever forget it?"

"I haven't come here to bring back your paltry memories."

"The balance has broken down, and the whole thing is out of control."

"Do you want to be put back on a firm basis again?"

"With all the strength I have."

"Fine. Focus your thoughts carefully and answer the questions I ask you honestly."

"You'll find I'll do anything you want, Father."

"I'm not your father!" he yelled.

"Not my father?!"

"The fact that you think that's the case shows you're still living in the stone age!"

"But that's a genuine relationship which no one denies."

"No, it's a special relationship which prevents you from having a real sense of vision."

He felt he should go along with him rather than argue. "I apologize for my mistake," he said. " I made it inadvertently."

"Tell me, what was the most important thing which happened to you when you were a child?"

"I can't remember. My childhood may have gone by without anything which was worth remembering."

"That's a stupid, blind answer; it suggests that the consequences will be fatuous."

"I really...."

"Tell me, what was the biggest sin you committed in your youth?"

He got ready, but did not answer.

"You're still ashamed of something which you needn't be ashamed of," the man said. " That suggests you're proud of things you should be ashamed of...."

"I'm sorry...."

"Tell me, how many people have you killed?"

"I haven't killed anyone, thank God."

"Hasn't anyone thought about killing you?"

"Certainly not! What makes you think such things about me?"

The father sighed audibly.

"I've lived a good life," the man continued."

"Good!"

"Spoiled only by some minor mistakes like...."

"I'm not interested in hearing about minor mistakes."

"I've rendered some significant services to society."

"Significant!"

"What are you really bothered about, Father?"

"'Father' again!"

"Sorry!"

"A whole life wasted."

"What do you want me to do?"

"What a complete waste when a meeting ends up with the same question it started with!"

"But you didn't say anything...."

"I said everything...."

The father disappeared without his even laying eyes on him. Nevertheless he was aware that he had gone and felt bitterly frustrated. However, that did not last long. He found himself tending to believe his father when he had declared that he had said everything. All he had to do was to remember what he had said. He started trying to remember. "This birthday isn't like the previous ones," he thought. " My head's spinning around, and as it spins, it's scattering all the thoughts inside. Everything's flying around."

He tried to remember, but he was thwarted by the nurse's arrival. They shook hands warmly, and he looked at her as she was preparing the needle, admiring her youthful freshness. He took off his jacket and rolled up his shirt sleeve. He gave her his arm and she gave him the injection. "I hope you'll get well...." she said.

"Thank you."

She put the needle back in the sterilizing box.

"Stay here and join in my birthday party," he said.

"I don't know any of the guests," she replied.

"Two men and their wives. No one else is left!"

"I haven't brought a present."

"You are the present...."

"I'm not properly dressed," she said, pointing at her modest work coat.

"We're all in our seventies and eighties, so you can be our connection with the present."

She hesitated somewhat.

"I won't let you go," he said, holding her by the wrist. With a smile she sat down on the chair next to his.

"Is everything okay?" he asked.

"Thank God, yes," she replied.

"When are you getting married?"

"At the end of next month."

"I shall miss you a lot...."

"Aren't you satisfied yet?"

She laughed. He smiled back although there was a certain amount of insipidness in his smile. The guests arrived, two friends and their wives. The presents were laid out on the table and they kissed each other; laughter echoed forth. The ladies and gentlemen were introduced to the nurse, and then the man filled up the glasses himself even though the old servant was standing behind the bar. Jokes and stories were all mixed in with the congratulations. The man himself applied half of his mind to the conversation and seemed serious and thoughtful in spite of attempts to conceal it. He did not sit down like his guests, but started pacing up and down and then stopping.

"Sit down," the first friend said, "it's disturbing us to see you standing up."

"Why won't you sit down?" the other friend's wife asked.

He gave an enigmatic smile. "Something tells me," he said, "that this will be my last birthday."

"No, God forbid!" said more than one voice.

"You'll see I'm telling the truth," he said emphatically.

"What's the matter with you?" the first friend asked.

"You're not your usual self," his wife said. She turned towards the nurse. "Is everything okay?" she asked.

"He's in the best of health," the young girl replied.

"Then render to God the things that are God's," the other friend suggested. "Sit down and celebrate your birthday."

"No!"

"No?"

"I've decided I have to do my duty."

"What duty?"

"Before the opportunity is lost forever."

"It's the whiskey, that's all!"

"This is no time for stupid jokes."

"But it's your birthday."

"Our friend's charming, that's all," said the second friend's wife.

The man moved over to the other side of the room, rested his foot on a chair and put his weight on it. He started looking at them carefully, staring at them one by one. "Time is passing," he said, "and you are getting old. You must face the advancing years fair and square."

"Cheers!" said the first friend with a laugh, raising his glass as he did.

"I have a piece of prose poetry," said the wife of the other friend. "When will you let me recite it?"

"No one will talk tonight except me," the man replied looking serious.

"But it's your birthday!"

"The last one!"

"Let's stop this distressing conversation!"

"Listen. I've attended a judicial deliberation, and now I've been authorized to carry out the enquiry, verdict and execution!"

"I bet this will all turn out to he a marvellous joke!"

"I doubt that very much."

"I suggest we go along with him to the end." the first friend said.

"Fine," said the other friend. "Just consider us as standing before your court!"

"That's the way you are, whether you like it or not."

"What do you want with us?"

"I said that time is passing and people are getting old. You have to face facts fair and square."

"Then let's have it."

"Tell me," he said, pointing at the two men, "how many

people have you killed?"

They burst out laughing. He waited till they stopped. "Tell me," he continued when they were quiet again, "Why haven't you been in prison at least?"

"There!" said the other friend's wife, "didn't I say it would turn out to be a marvellous joke?"

"I'm authorized to kill anyone who hasn't killed, been killed or imprisoned."

"You enemy of all that's good!" yelled the other friend.

"Tell us then," said the first friend, "when did you kill someone? When were you killed or when did you go to prison?"

"Don't we deserve to be killed as well?" the wife of the first friend asked with a laugh.

"You never spoke a truer word, Madam," the man said roughly.

"Really?!"

"Have you forgotten the love we shared when we were young?"

For the first time, the atmosphere changed. People frowned in dismay.

"Have you lost your mind?" the first friend yelled angrily. "Where are your manners?"

"There's no avoiding the truth," the man said obstinately. "Our love was real, but it so happened that you were her cousin and they said you had priority when it came to marrying her. Then she broke down and gave in."

"You're crazy. Explain what you're getting at...."

"She broke down and gave in. She didn't resist, and then she gave in again afterwards. I admit to you that we – she and I – joined together in deceiving you for about five years."

The first friend leapt to his feet, and was about to pounce on the man, but the latter drew a revolver out of his pocket, pointed it at him and fired. The friend fell to the ground amid a chorus of screams. Even the old servant screamed.

"Everyone stay where they are!" the man yelled with the

revolver in his shaking hand.

The friend's wife threw herself on her husband sobbing hysterically.

"Why are you crying?" he asked with a leer. "You married him in spite of yourself and betrayed him through your own will. How hideous it is to see tears running down your cheeks. Do you want to join him?"

"Criminal...mad fool!..." she yelled angrily, but a bullet settled in her neck before she could finish the sentence and she sank to the floor alongside her husband, her body smeared with his blood.

The other people stared at him in dazed amazement.

"You must acknowledge that killing is the greatest challenge in life's prison bars," he said.

"What's happened to you, my dear friend?" said the other friend in an uncontrolled voice. "Have you forgotten that we came here to celebrate your birthday?!"

"You too," he said, retrieving his consciousness from the echoes of the conversation, "you've never killed anyone either...."

"Just like millions of other people," the friend replied in panic. "Otherwise there wouldn't be anyone left on the earth. What's happened to you, my dear friend?"

"We're your friends," his wife said trembling. "Have you forgotten our long friendship and half a century's affection?!"

"You as well!" he said, looking at her in contempt. "You only married him for his money. You gave in as well. None of you has any respect for resistance!"

"Are you passing judgment on me for childish emotions my heart felt half a century ago?"

"I know your lover too!"

"God forgive you!"

"Let us go," the friend pleaded.

"Why don't you get angry about your family honor?" the man asked derisively.

"By our lifelong friendship, please let us go!"

"We've reached a point where we can't retreat."

"Are you going to kill innocent people as a whole?"

"No one is innocent."

The nurse hid her face between her hands.

"Fear God Almighty, Sir...." the old servant behind the bar yelled.

"Well done, old man," he said joyfully. He fired the revolver twice, and the friend and his wife both fell to the ground. All that could be heard was the beautiful nurse sobbing. He looked towards her. "Why did you accept the invitation, you unlucky girl?"

She carried on sobbing without replying. .

"Maybe your conscience enticed you into accepting," he said.

"I did it to show my respect for you," she said with a sob.

"But you loathe me like death," he said in a tone full of hatred.

"Me?"

"Yes."

"Don't misjudge me."

"Once I snatched a glance in the mirror while we were embracing and I could see repulsion written all over your face like tar!"

"Never, never...."

"One day, I offered to take you as my wife, but you made excuses...."

"You know very well, I was engaged...."

"Yes. The real truth was that I respected you...."

"It was just that I was engaged...."

"You were quite prepared to be my mistress and earn some money to help you prepare yourself for getting married...."

"Sir...."

"You didn't resist! What makes you all hate resistance?"

"At any rate, you were quite happy about my decision."

"That's true, and that's why I condemn you to death."

The beautiful girl leapt up to try to save herself, but the

bullet was too quick for her. She fell to the ground face downwards. He took his foot off the chair and moved slowly forward, looking at the corpses. He looked over at the old servant behind the bar who looked as pale as death.

"Dear old man," he said, "What do you think about what you've seen?"

The servant couldn't say a word.

"You started serving me as a young man," he continued, "and now here you are standing there like a dry withered branch...."

The old man shook his head without saying anything.

"How much you've suffered at my hands on occasions...."

"Sir...."

"And it never occurred to you once to leave my house...."

"In spite of everything, you were kind-hearted."

"Don't lie. You've been embroiled in many different things with me here, some decent, others indecent. You've seen all kinds of utter debauchery here!"

"In spite of that, I can't forget your good points."

"You never once thought of treating me as I deserved?"

"Sir, I'm your obedient servant."

"That's why I condemn you to death...."

The old man tried to hide behind the bar, but the bullet pierced his head. The man sighed deeply; he sighed deeply till it filled the whole room...."

◆ ◆ ◆ ◆

He felt the light shining through his closed eyelids, and opened his eyes. He saw the old servant standing there and the room bathed in light. He got up from his comfortable chair. "Have the guests arrived?" he asked.

"No, but the nurse has come...."

The servant went out, and the nurse entered beaming. They exchanged broad smiles. He took off his jacket and rolled up his sleeve while she prepared the injection.

"Happy birthday!" she said.

"I'd like to invite you to a little party," he said, giving her his arm.

"I'd love to," she replied, wiping the pinprick with a piece of cotton moistened with alcohol, "But I have a date with my fiance."

"He's invited too. I hope you'll tell him so."

"He'll be delighted to accept your invitation. He hasn't forgotten that you helped him transfer to Cairo. But he's not too well...."

"Is he ill?"

"Oh no! It's just that he's not in good shape psychologically...."

"That'll pass. When are you getting married?"

"Soon at any rate."

"I shall miss you a great deal."

"Careful!" she replied with a laugh, "I'm starting a new life when I get married!"

"What a charming opportunist you are! I'll never forget the happiness I've found at your hands!"

"Congratulations once again."

She left. As she went out, he followed her with his eyes and then looked around at the room; the floor, the chairs and the bar. He sighed deeply and then looked at the time. "A really long journey!" he muttered, " at least in a space of five minutes!"

He started pacing up and down the hall, but that did not last for long. The guests soon arrived; two men and women in their seventies and eighties. The presents were laid out on the table and they exchanged kisses. They all took their seats and the man proceeded to fill their glasses himself.

"We're the only ones left."

"God have mercy on the departed!"

"I've got an important announcement to make," said the wife of the first friend, "in the hope of keeping our precious conversation palatable."

"What's that?"

"That we avoid talking politics or war."

"A very sensible idea."

"It drains all our energy and turns any pleasant conversation sour. It always leads to an impasse. So let's spare ourselves tonight...."

"I doubt very much whether we can carry through with this simple suggestion. We'll pretend to be following it and start talking about this and that but then, before we know it, we'll be at the front again...."

"Even if we choose some topic or other and stick to it, we'll soon find the conversation meaningless and without any pith to it. In reality, we're running away from the one topic of conversation we are bound to talk about. Eventually there'll be no alternative but to go back to the front. Opinions and probabilities will branch out in all directions, and the canons of war and peace will again be in conflict. We'll spend the night drowning in a trap which we've dug with our own hands...."

"Then I'll appoint myself guardian angel over the evening's chatter," the woman said with determination. "I'll sound the alarm whenever I sense that the conversation is drifting towards the eternal topic."

"A pretty good experiment; but I predict it'll fail before you even start...."

"Your health."

"And yours too."

"But why is our birthday host looking so distracted?"

"Me?"

"Yes...something is going on inside that noble head of yours...."

"The fact is," he said with a laugh, "that I had a strange dream...."

"A nice one, I hope."

"What can I say?"

"Tell us what you saw and we'll be able to interpret it for you."

"I dreamed that I shot you all," he said, looking at them peculiarly.

Everyone burst out laughing.

"That's marvellous! We're like old horses being shot out of kindness."

"I felt utterly delighted as I was shooting you all...."

"Dreams can be interpreted to mean their exact opposite. This dream means that you're wishing us a long life."

"Fine."

"If we rely on science to help us to interpret it, Freud for example, we'll discover suppressed sexual urges in you which are better not disclosed...."

"It wouldn't have been possible for me to keep them hidden all this time."

"Your health."

"And yours too."

"Even the women?"

"Yes, I killed them too!"

"Such close friends, and yet...."

"Even the old servant and the nurse!?"

"It wasn't a dream, but a continuation of talk about war."

"Perhaps."

"Why did you do us the favor of killing us?"

"I can't remember any more. Details of dreams are soon forgotten."

"Can you remember why you did it? It must be really peculiar."

"I don't think so...."

"We must have provoked you in some way?"

"Maybe."

"What did you do after you had finished us off?"

"I can't remember."

"Did you feel sorry?"

"I don't think so."

"Allow me to say...."

But the servant came in to announce that the nurse and

her fiance had arrived. The servant went out, and the nurse came in followed by her fiance. The man made the introductions, and the two newcomers sat next to each other. The young man was smiling affectionately as though he might be trying to hide some feeling of depression which he could not keep hidden. The man brought them over two glasses. "Your health!" he said.

"We're grateful to you both for coming," said the first friend, "our conversation needs some new blood...."

"She's a marvellous young woman," the man said, "and he's a young man of considerable talent, but he doesn't look too well."

"I'm feeling fine, Sir," the young man replied.

"Really? What do you think, young lady?"

"He is just as you say, Sir," she replied a little sadly, "But we shouldn't spoil the fun of the party with our troubles...."

"Is he ill?" the second friend asked.

"No, Sir, but from time to time he's plagued by an obscure feeling of impending doom...."

"How can anyone feel like that when he has you as his fiancee?"

"I'm fine," the young man said in protest.

"You're not...." the man said.

"Sir, it's not right to worry you with our problems."

"Be frank with me, my son; I'm playing the role of your father."

"Perhaps what you tell us will take our minds off another topic of conversation which has been haunting us," said the first friend's wife.

"What's causing your troubles?" the second friend asked.

"There's no cause...." the nurse replied.

"A disagreement at work perhaps?" the first friend asked.

"No, nothing at all," the young man replied.

"Maybe it's a sign of anxiety, the kind of thing lovers feel?"

"No, nothing at all, Sir."

The nurse couldn't stop herself. "On our way here," she said, "he told me that suicide was a fine idea!"

"Why are you repeating something I said without any purpose or meaning?" the young man asked her.

"I was really afraid...."

"What strange moods you have...."

"I'm sorry."

"We're spoiling the atmosphere here...."

"Don't worry, my son," the old man said. "I dreamt a little while ago that I killed all my guests including your fiancee and even the old servant...."

The guests burst into laughter. Even the young man smiled.

"Drink up," the man said, "and forget about your worries. Believe me, I offer you a special welcome. I can feel you're sharing my peculiar situation with me...."

Then he turned towards his friends. "Excuse me," he said. "I think I have some good things to tell our young friend here. So go ahead and have a good time...."

"I'm looking forward to some really unusual conversation which will be worth following up," the first friend said, "particularly because it won't stop us eating and drinking!"

"It's your fault," the man said, looking at the nurse. "How could you let him drown in troubles like that?"

"I thought we were happy," she replied. "That, at any rate, is what I believed...."

"Why are you feeling miserable?" the man asked the young man.

"She's exaggerating, Sir."

"I've never exaggerated," the nurse replied.

"We're on the thirty-fifth floor," the man said, "and that has taught me some sense...."

"Does that have anything to do with murdering us?" the second friend asked with a laugh.

The man took the young man by the hand and took him

over to the window. "We're really high up here," he said, "you can see more than one Nile flowing in Cairo...."

"A really incredible view," the young man replied. "It must be even better in the daytime...."

"From here, the gardens look like tiny engineering diagrams drawn on a piece of paper...."

"Perhaps...but I hope you don't believe that I was really thinking of suicide."

"Cars look like children's toys, people seem like mice, mountains and houses are an incredible continuously expanding structure with domes and minarets popping up here and there, roads vanish altogether and so do people as individuals. You can't tell them apart. There's no sign of their worries, problems or happiness."

"How incredible it all is!"

"It's wonderful to deal with the sun, the wind and height! Is my conversation bothering you?"

"No, no. I'm afraid that my presence here may be bothering you."

"Raise your voice a little, my dear," said the first friend's wife.

"We need the benefit of your good words too!"

"I'm pleased with you," the man said to the young man. "Maybe I can convince you, just as I have done myself, to live above everything!"

"Above everything?"

"I mean that you should look at your troubles from above, just as you are looking down at the city now. You can view them as abstract shapes, and they have no effect on you!"

"Very good, philosopher!" yelled the second friend.

"That idea has often occurred to people with problems who are looking for consolation," the young man replied, "but it has no basis in truth."

"It's a description based on experience," the wife of the second friend said to the young man, " so don't look down on it, my dear."

"Yes...," the man said, "don't look down on it. How marvellous to live above everything!"

"But we were created to live down there."

"Can't you come up here?"

"I don't think so. Millions of people are struggling down there below us...."

"That doesn't alter the essential truth...."

"That I doubt, Sir...."

The man pointed to the city dotted with lights. "Here and there, things are happening," he said. "Relationships come into being, quarrels erupt. But to anyone looking out from this window, nothing is happening at all!"

"Maybe that's just because we're short-sighted, Sir!"

"Youth is a dangerous phase in life. It refuses to make truces and despises wisdom. As a result, there are only two courses before it, suicide or revolution...."

"Isn't love another course?" the first friend asked.

"Suicide or revolution?" the young man asked.

"And they're both the same for anyone looking out of this window."

"The window!"

"You sound sarcastic! Tell me truthfully why you came here tonight."

"To join in the birthday celebration...."

"What else?"

"Perhaps I was also looking for some relaxation."

"That's a bad sign."

"Why bad?"

"It shows that you're floundering in problems."

"Life is never free of them."

"The important thing is the stand we take in life, isn't it?"

"We should carry on the struggle."

"Please don't repeat memorized slogans in my presence."

"I'm not ashamed of repeating slogans if they're true...."

"I'm a man of experience, and I've won myself a victory

over this world. I must divulge my secret to anyone who needs it...."

"Thank you."

"Don't you believe me?"

"I'm longing to know your secret."

"We're eager to hear it too," said more than one voice.

"In the beginning, there were anxieties," the man said.

"In the beginning?"

"When I started the experiment*, I felt weighed down with anxieties."

"What anxieties, if you please?"

"That's not important. Discord, disobedience, filth, the country's problems, earthquakes in Yugoslavia. Don't bother about names; anxieties were weighing me down."

"And then?"

"I felt utterly weary and oppressed. Then one day, I found myself looking down on the city from this window. At that moment, the truth came to me all at once...."

"The truth?"

"That anxieties didn't exist at all."

"Where did they disappear?"

"All I could see was a city, a mere city."

"The city itself will vanish if you go up high enough."

"Just an abstract city with no sign of any anxieties."

"Pure fancy."

"Never."

"The fact is that anxieties are buried deep down inside us."

"But they vanish if you look from above...."

"Impossible."

"I've done just that, I've won."

"Do you mean that nothing makes you sad any longer?"

"Certainly."

"That means you're no longer human."

---

* The Arabic word conveys the dual meaning of 'experiment', and 'test/ordeal'.

"I warn you again not to repeat slogans."

"But it's the truth."

"The only truth is my triumphant experiment."

"Imagine – God forbid – that you lost the thing you hold most dear to you."

"I've tried even worse than that. I challenge you to differentiate between grave and home in your present position...."

"That's just intellectual consolation; it has nothing to do with feelings."

"Feelings eventually give in to the window."

"I don't believe you...."

"You must believe him," the second friend's wife said.

"It means you're no longer alive," the young man said to the man.

"Or else that I'm living above life's pinnacle."

"Perhaps you don't realize how greedy real life is."

"I was kneaded and baked in it."

"Then you're the happiest man in the world."

"We're talking about philosophy, not happiness."

"Maybe you're a philosopher, but – unfortunately – you're not alive."

"I'm still breathing."

"Your philosophy is liable to kill off the motives for real life."

"Now we've returned to slogans again."

"By killing progress."

"I've never failed to do my duty."

"And you never did any duty, did you?"

"You're throwing riddles at me, aren't you?"

"You're beginning to understand me...."

"But what you're saying goes against reality. It seems complicated and unintelligible."

"What you've just said can be applied to anything in life."

"I'm sorry I can't profit from your philosophy...."

"I admit that I was worried when I first looked at you."

"Why?"

"Something told me you might be thinking of something dangerous!"

"What's that?"

I admit that I've thought of suicide too...."

"A thought far from reality, as remote as the distance from this window to the ground...."

"That's why I let you into the secret which stifles any thought of suicide."

"Thank you. I don't need it. Furthermore, I have my own special ways."

"Fine.... Go back to your seat and have a drink."

Everyone was ready for various comments. The man stayed where he was in front of the window and then stood on a nearby chair. Everyone was thunderstruck.

"Are you thinking of giving a speech?" the first friend asked.

From that position, he moved on to the window sill, with considerable lightness considering his age. There he stood leaning on each side of the window frame with his two hands. Everyone stood up in confusion.

"What are you doing?" said more than one voice. "Be careful...."

Next moment, they saw him throw himself into space. He disappeared rapidly leaving behind him a strangled cry like a wolf howling.

بابل بين باب النزولية وباب النخل

The Prisoner of War's Uniform

When it was nearly time for trains to arrive at the station in Zagazig, Gahsha, the cigarette seller, was always the first to rush there. He rightly regarded the station as his most profitable market. He would walk along the platform with an unrivalled energy, looking for customers with his small experienced eyes. Maybe if Gahsha had been asked about his job, he would have uttered a foul curse; for, like most people, he was fed up with his life and unhappy with his own lot. If he had had the freedom of choice, he might have preferred to be some rich person's chauffeur. Then he could have worn *efendi's* clothes* and eaten the Bey's food, he could have accompanied him to exclusive places during the summer and winter. He preferred something which would divert him and keep him amused rather than have to struggle to get his food.

However, he also had his own special reasons and pretexts for preferring that kind of job and wanting it so much. These dated from the day when he noticed Alghur, the chauffeur of one of the local notables, standing in the way of Nabawiyya, the *ma'mur's* servant, and flirting with her in a brash and self-confident fashion. He once even heard him tell her as he rubbed his hands with glee that he would soon be back with the ring. Then Gahsha saw the girl smile at Alghur flirtatiously and lift the edge of her *milaya**** away from her face as though she were adjusting it. The truth was that she wanted to show off her jet-black hair greased with

* i.e. western dress.
** shawl, usually black

oil.... When Gahsha saw it, his heart caught fire. He felt envy gnawing away painfully inside him. Her black eyes caused him all manner of pain and suffering. He would follow a few paces behind her; sometimes, he would stand in her way when he saw her walking along the street. Eventually, when he got her alone in an alley, he would repeat what Alghur had said about bringing the ring. But she would turn away and frown. "It would make more sense if you got yourself some clogs," she would reply disdainfully. He would stare at his huge feet which looked as though they were lined with camels' hooves, at his dirty *gallabiyya* and his dusty skullcap. "That's why I'm so miserable," he told himself, "that's why my star has set." He envied Alghur his job, the one he wanted so much. Nevertheless, these hopes of his did not prevent him from working, and he set about his job tenaciously, finding the fulfillment of his hopes in dreams.

That afternoon, he made for the station carrying his tray and waited for the train to arrive. He looked towards the horizon and saw the train coming in the distance like a cloud of smoke. It came nearer and nearer, and the different parts of it could be made out more clearly. The noise became louder and louder, and eventually it came to a halt in the station.

Gahsha hurried up to the crowded carriages and noticed to his amazement that there were armed guards at the doors and strange faces peering out through the windows with dazed and downtrodden expressions. When people asked about the train, they were told that the men were Italian prisoners of war who had fallen into enemy hands in countless numbers and were now being transferred to prison camps.

Gahsha stood there in bewilderment as he surveyed the dusty faces. He began to feel dejected because he realized that these people with pale faces which reflected their despair and poverty would not be able to satisfy their craving for his cigarettes.... He noticed them avidly devouring his tray with their eyes, and looked at them in angry derision. He was about to turn round and go back the way he had come when he heard someone shouting at him in Arabic with a European accent 'Cigarette'. He stared at the man doubtfully and then rubbed his index finger with his thumb to show that he wanted money. The soldier understood what he meant and nodded. Gahsha came over cautiously and stood far enough away so that the soldier could not reach him. The soldier took off his jacket quietly and pointed at it. "This is my money," he said.

Gahsha was astonished and eyed the grey jacket with its yellow buttons with a mixture of bewilderment and longing. His heart was throbbing, but he was no simpleton or fool and kept well hidden any feelings which might have let him fall prey to the Italian's greed. With an outward display of calm, he produced a box of cigarettes and stretched out his arm to take the jacket. The soldier frowned. "One box for a jacket!" he yelled. "Give me ten of them!" At this, Gahsha became alarmed and moved back; his longing had dwindled somewhat. He was about to leave again. "Give me a decent number." the soldier yelled, "nine or eight." The young man shook his head stubbornly. "Seven then!" the soldier said. He shook his head again and pretended to be making up his mind to leave. The soldier said he would be happy with six, and then came down to five. Gahsha gestured with his hand and made a show of despair, then retreated to a seat and sat down. "Come over here," the demented soldier yelled, "I'll take four...."Gahsha paid no attention, and just to show how unconcerned he was, he lit a cigarette and started smoking it with a quiet relish. The soldier flew into a rage and lost his temper completely. The only goal of his existence, it seemed, was to get hold of cigarettes. He brought his demands down to three, then to two. Gahsha remained in his seat; his emotions were burning inside him and his longing for the jacket was hurting, but he still controlled himself. When the soldier came down to two boxes. Gahsha let slip an involuntary movement which the soldier noticed. "Come on," the soldier said, holding out the jacket. Gahsha saw that there was nothing for it but to get up, go over to the train, take the jacket and hand over the two boxes to the soldier. He eyed the jacket with glee and delight; a smile of victory showed on his lips. He put the tray down on the seat, put the jacket on and buttoned it up. It looked too big on him, but he did not care about that. He felt so proud of himself and happy.

He picked up his tray again and began to walk along the platform full of pride and joy. In his mind's eye he could see a picture of Nabawiyya wrapped up in her *milaya*. "If only she could see me now," he muttered. "Yes indeed, she won't shun me anymore after today or turn away in disdain. Alghur won't find anything to boast about at my expense." Then he remembered that Alghur wore a complete suit, not just a jacket. How could he get hold of some trousers? He thought for a moment, and looked meaningfully at the heads of the prisoners of war leaning out of the windows. Longing played with his heart once again, and he began to get excited just as he was about to calm down. He walked towards the train. "Cigarettes, cigarettes," he yelled out brashly, " a box for a pair of trousers." He repeated this a second and third time. He was afraid that the soldiers did not understand what he meant, so he started pointing at the jacket he was wearing and gesturing with a box of cigarettes. This produced the desired effect. One soldier did not hesitate for a moment but started to take off his jacket. Gahsha hurried towards him and gestured to him to stop. He pointed at his trousers to show him that they were what he wanted. The soldier shrugged his shoulders as if he did not particularly care. He took off his trousers, and the exchange was completed. Gahsha grabbed the trousers feeling almost beside himself with glee. He went back to his seat and began to put the trousers on. In less than a minute, he had finished and become a complete Italian soldier.... Was anything missing, I wonder? It was really unfortunate that the prisoners did not cover their heads with *tarbushes*, but they did have shoes on their feet. He had to have some shoes so that he could be on equal terms with Alghur, the one person who was ruining his life for him.

He picked up his tray again and hurried towards the train. "Cigarettes," he yelled, "a box for some shoes...a box for some shoes." He started making gestures as he had done last time so that they could understand what he meant. But, before he could find a new customer, the whistle sounded to announce the train's departure. This led to a surge of activity which involved all the guards. Darkness was beginning to hide parts of the station, and the bird of night was hovering in the air. Gahsha stood there feeling heart-broken with a look of sorrowful anger in his eyes. When the train started to move, one of the guards in a front carriage spotted him. He looked furious and yelled at him in English and then Italian. "Get on the train at once," he shouted. "Hey you, prisoner!" Gahsha did not understand what he was saying and felt like venting his own feelings. So he began to imitate the guard's actions and mock him; he was convinced that the guard was too far away to grab hold of him. The guard yelled again as the train was drawing further and further away.

"Get on the train," he shouted, "I'm warning you...get on at once!"

Gahsha tightened his lips in derision and turned his back on the guard. He was about to leave. The guard clenched his fist threateningly and then aimed his rifle at the stupid young man...he fired. The deafening shot rang out, and it was followed by a scream of agony. Gahsha's body was crucified where he stood, the tray fell from his hand, and the boxes of cigarettes and matches were scattered over the platform. Then he rolled over onto his face, a lifeless corpse.

An Unnerving Sound

He sat there in his usual morning seat at the Tree Casino sipping coffee and smoking a cigarette. He was either looking at the still waters of the Nile or else upwards at the clear July sky, the color of which faded in the intense sunshine. He had some uneasy thoughts, closed his eyes to concentrate, and then opened them again. He noticed his notebook open at a white page and his pencil thrown across it at his beck and call. Looking around the rest of the cafe, he saw two people here and two others there, but they were the only ones. Even the waiter was sitting on the wall overlooking the Nile having a sort of holiday. He was the only one who came to this place to do any work; he had come on this stubborn and recalcitrant July day to look for some inspiration for a new topic to fill his column *Yesterday and Today* in his weekly magazine. And this topic had to be something new week after week, and so it went on forever. His whole happiness depended on his success in this work, his nice apartment, his wife, his baby who was almost two years old, his Opel car, not to mention his bachelor place in the East building which was available for unforeseen requirements.

"Heavens, be generous with your ideas...."

He looked through his glasses at a palace on the other bank of the river directly opposite where he was sitting. The windows and doors were locked, and the walls gleamed brightly in the sunlight, but there was no movement anywhere; even the trees were still and looked as solid as statues.

"Oh, to live in a palace! No bother about earning a

living, no worries except just thinking!"

He looked at the dregs in the bottom of his coffee cup. "I have ideas and projects," he told himself with a sigh, "but I waste my entire life recording various observations and proposing familiar solutions to familiar problems. Ugh...."

"Professor Adham," said a gentle voice from behind which startled him, "good morning...."

He turned round with a smile so as to hide the shock he felt and then released himself from his thoughts. "Nadra," he said, "how nice to see you."

They shook hands, and she sat down opposite him, putting her handbag on top of the white page. "I saw your back from the road," she said, "and recognized you."

"When will you recognize me from the front as well as from the back?"

"Your face is imprinted in my heart," she replied jokingly.

All the time, he was looking at her svelte figure and face which gleamed with a spirit of youth. Even though childhood and adolescence were still close together in her life, she had make-up on her face, her eyes, eyelids, brows and lashes and nails.

"Were you on your way to or from an appointment?" he asked without bothering about her little joke.

"I don't like morning appointments. I was dithering around in the car with no particular purpose in mind."

No purpose! Infectious terminology! But you're thirty-five and she's seventeen. She is free enough to arouse the interest of any married man with a bachelor place of his own. She reads a lot and is very fond of Francoise Sagan. She had certainly surprised him on the night when he had first met her along with a group of friends in *Sans Souci*. She could comment on life in an extraordinary way and, when necessary, did not mind cracking a dirty joke. She had been studying scenario since abandoning her university studies; maybe she was striving for the stars. She had written several artistic pieces but, in spite of her beauty, she had failed to get them published in magazines or broadcasts. When they had last met, she had declared in the presence of some friends how much she admired atheist existentialism!

"What can I order for you?" he asked, and then carried on in a semi-serious tone, "or would you prefer us to postpone that till we go to my private apartment?"

"Order some coffee and stop dreaming...."

He offered her a cigarette and lit it for her. She started drinking the coffee without bothering about the way he was staring at her.

"How's the existential anxiety?!" he eventually asked jokingly.

"Fine. But I only slept for two hours yesterday."

"Thought and philosophy?"

"A row with Mother and Father as you can imagine."

With a start he remembered the topic he was looking into seriously.

"Finish your education," she continued, imitating her parents' tone of voice. "Get married...don't play around as young men do...."

A typical recording, but the girl was beautiful and the session was proving inspiring. Who knows?! However he had to finish today's topic even if it meant cancelling his evening appointments. "How do you expect them to understand a little philosopher like you?" he asked.

A frown warned him against proceeding any farther with that kind of joking.

"No one's prepared to admit," she said, "that I'm struggling to create myself, but I'm living with the People of the Cave!"*

He remembered that her father had expressed his ideas more than once on television. "But your father's a man of the times," he said.

"Man of the times!"

---

* A group of people associated with 'The Seven Sleepers of Bphesus', a story partially related in the Qur'an, Sura 18.

"Compared with my father at least."

"Compared with the stone age perhaps?" she replied suppressing a laugh.

He looked into the distance as though he were dreaming.

"The stone age!" he said with fascination. "If only we could go back to that period just for an hour, I would carry you off on my shoulder with no one to stop me and take you to my cave in the East Building!"

"I told you to stop dreaming," she said. "Let me tell you why I've come...."

"Oh! So we didn't meet by chance then?"

"You know that I know that you spend every morning here writing."

"Then let's go to the East Building," he said in mock seriousness, "so that we can find a suitable place to talk seriously!"

"Can't you see I'm not joking?" she said, lighting one cigarette with another. She fixed him with her piercing eyes as pure as honey. "You promised me once," she continued, "that you'd introduce me to Mr. Ali al-Kabir."

"Are you serious?" he asked anxiously.

"Absolutely."

"No doubt, you admire him as an actor!"

"Of course...."

They looked at each other.

"He's forty-five!" he said.

"I know. Have you heard about the magic of time?"

"No. But I've heard a lot about the tragedy of time."

"You set yourself up as some kind of moral counsellor in *Yesterday and Today*. But here...."

"What's my part in the story?"

"You're his best friend."

"He has a daughter your age."

"That's right. I think she's at law school...."

"Tell me what's on your mind," he said after thinking for a while. "Are you thinking for example of destroying his family life and then marrying him?"

"I'm not thinking of any such thing," she replied letting out a laugh.

"Just love then?"

She shrugged her shoulders without saying anything.

"A quick way to a screen part?" he asked.

"I'm not an opportunist," she replied disdainfully.

"Well then?!"

"You must keep your promise."

Suddenly he had an idea.

"You've given me the inspiration for a topic!" he shouted.

"What is it?"

"Free love, yesterday and today," he replied after a moment's thought.

"Tell me more."

He felt himself impelled by an urge which he made no attempt to dislodge. "Take an example on the subject," he said. "In olden times, when a girl went wrong, she was said to be a fallen woman; whereas now they say it's anxiety caused by civilization or else philosophical anxiety."

"You're antediluvian," she said angrily, "even though you pretend to be forward-looking."

"What do you expect from someone whose ancestors lived in the stone age?"

"Can't you look at me as a human being who's like you in every way?"

"If you were narcissistic, yes."

"There you are making fun of me, and my father yells at me."

"What about you?"

"I'm still asking you to keep your promise."

"Let me give you some idea about him first. He's a great artist; in many people's view, he's the foremost film actor. He has a familiar policy which he never changes. If he's introduced to a girl like you, he takes her straightway to his private house near the Pyramid, and then begins where other people leave off."

"I'm grateful for your kind advice."

"You still want to meet him?"

"Certainly...?"

"Fine," he said provocatively. "But I must ask for the cost in advance!"

She moved her head to show that she did not understand. That dislodged a strand of black hair which curled in a circle over her eyebrow.

"I'd like you to pay me a visit at the East Building."

She smiled without saying anything or indeed believing he was being serious.

"Agreed?"

"I'm sure your mind is cleaner than that."

"I'm afflicted by the anxiety of the age!"

"No, no. Don't mix jokes and serious discussion. I've wasted your valuable time," she said apologetically.

She lit a third cigarette, and they looked at each other for a long while. They smiled together. He started thinking about his topic again. The atmosphere had been totally cleared of any misunderstanding, and an oppressive feeling of heat and humidity had returned.

"You're a reactionary in trendy clothing!" she said jokingly.

"No, I'm not! You're not being frank with yourself. But you're really delightful, and your jokes are fun. I'll arrange the meeting in my office at the magazine; drop in – quite by accident – on Wednesday evening at nine."

"Thanks."

"I owe you my thanks for next week's article."

"I'll see how you deal with it."

"When I'm writing, I become a totally different personality!"

"You stick to some preordained pattern or other which has to be followed, even if it means going against what you really feel."

"Perhaps. The truth is that the best of me hasn't

expressed itself yet."

When she noticed him looking at the notebook, she stopped arguing with him and put her handbag on an empty chair. He looked once more at the sleepy palace deep in its cloistered magnificence. He liked the balcony adjoining the garden and admired even more the balcony on the higher floor resting on pillars which looked like obelisks. How nice it would be to sit on that balcony in the moonlight, he thought, and be free to think without being bound by appointments and conventions; or to own a yacht and travel round on the ocean meeting people and seeing other countries with no boundaries and on condition that your wife stayed in Cairo; to play with roses in Hawaii and forget about the topics for *Yesterday and Today* and all the other problems like poverty, ignorance and disease. You have a certain amount of doubt about your own talents, but these sudden outbursts keep obscuring your doubt. They are strange, staggering outbursts which ignore any idea of rsponsibility, unintelligible, unquestionable and uncontrollable, but commentators from taverns and hashish rings keep volunteering to explain them.

"Nadra, what do you think of the absurd?" he asked.

"Very rational!" she replied enthusiastically.

"It's toying with me like a dream."

"I'm thinking of writing a theatre-of-the-absurd play for the puppet theatre," she said and then added with a sorrowful sigh, "if it weren't for my father, I would have written a crazy story about my experiences...."

"I wish you'd include me in those experiences!" he replied, not able to control his jocularity.

"Stop joking and think of the success they deserve." A delightful period of contemplation ensued, and they both lost themselves in a long period of silence.

Suddenly a sharp noise rang out which made them both start at the same time, a human voice shouting "Ho!" They saw a man tying up a boat with folded sails. It looked as though he were standing stock still, or else moving so very slowly and heavily as to be almost standing still. He was almost touching the outside of the wall just two metres away from where they were sitting and dragged the boat along with a long rope wrapped round his shoulders. Throwing himself forward, he flexed his muscles for all they were worth with great determination. The boat was moving slower than a turtle on the stagnant water in the still atmo-sphere. An old man wearing a *gallabiyya* and turban was standing in the bow and watching the other man struggle with a languid and sympathetic stare. The two of them sit--ting at the table no longer felt worried; anger had taken the place of anxiety, but neither of them said a word. The man carried on putting all his energy into his exhausting job till he was level with the spot where they were sitting. He was a young man in his twenties, dark-skinned, with swarthy fea-tures; he had nothing on his head or feet and was wearing a colorless *gallabiyya* with the top part open. The strain brought out all the varicose veins on his legs. His eyes bulged, his lips were taut, and he kept his back bent so as to avoid the scorching sun. Every time he felt exhausted, he would stop for a minute to take a deep breath.

"Heave ho!" the old man would yell.

"Ho!" he would yell in his turn.

His cruel struggle continued. In the minutes when he was alongside them, they could smell the stench of his body which reeked of sweat and mud. Their faces flinched, and Nadra put her delicate nose into a handkerchief impregnated with a beautiful scent. They both tried to pretend they were not disgusted and shocked as they watched the painful ordeal going on. They watched him move step by step till eventually this sharing in his task wore them both out. They turned away and looked at each other. With smiles of sympathy each of them lit a cigarette.

The Wilderness

It would be a savage, bloody battle. Twenty years of patient anticipation and waiting would be expunged. So be it! His eyes flashed with sparks as he walked on, surrounded by his aides. The line stretched out behind him; men holding knotted sticks, each one of them threatening to dig a deep trench in people's bones. As the procession had continued on its way, a group of people had joined them carrying baskets full of stones and pebbles. The men walked towards the desolate mountain with their wills poised for battle. It's the end for you Shardaha! From time to time, garbage collectors and undertakers would look at the procession and the man at the heart of it with curiosity, amazement and disapproval. Who was this new gang leader, they asked themselves, whom no one had ever seen before. You flies of creation, you'll recognize him and remember him by heart. You'll see! The setting sun with its warm rays shone over their colored skullcaps,and a crazy *khamsin* *wind was blowing, scorching people's faces and breathing gloominess and hate into the atmosphere.

One of the aides leaned over to the man. "Muallim Sharshara," he asked, "is Shardaha on the mountain road?"

"No. We must go through the Al-Jawwala quarter to get there."

"The news of our coming will fly there ahead of us. Your enemy will be waiting."

Sharshara frowned. "That's what I want," he said. "Treachery may succeed, but it won't expunge the revenge."

* desert wind

Twenty years of bitterness in exile, he thought to himself; far from watchful Cairo, buried in the unknown recesses of Alexandria port. Vengeance is the only hope in life. Food, drink, money, women, heaven and earth, they have all been immersed in clouds. His feelings were all focused on this painful process of preparation. Vengeance was the only idea he had; no love, no security, no desire to hang on to his money. Everything he possessed had been used up preparing for this fearsome day. That is how the flower of life dissolves into hatred, jealousy and grief. You weren't satisfied, he thought, with your slow, steady predominance over the workers in the port. You didn't reap any real fruit from your victory over the Ja'fars in the fights at Kum ad-Dikka. How easy it was to live as a thug whom everyone respected and to adopt Alexandria as a home with the name of Sharshara ringing out beneath the sky. But all your bloodshot eyes saw in the whole of existence was Shardaha with its narrow path, its zigzagging alley going up, and its foul, tyrannical thug, Lahluba...damn...damn!

The desert mountain road came to an end by the gate. The procession turned towards the crowded quarter of Al-Jawwala. "Don't talk to anyone or answer any questions," Sharshara yelled out in a commanding tone which sounded as sharp as an axe striking a rock.

Passers-by made way for the procession. People in taverns and cafes strained to get a look at them and stared for a long while at their new leader. Then they all felt scared and worried.

"They'll think we mean them some harm," his friend warned him.

Sharshara looked round at their sallow faces. "Men," he said audibly, "we mean you no harm."

People's faces relaxed, and greetings were exchanged.

"We're heading for Shardaha," he told them, look at his companion with a meaningful stare.

As he proceeded on his way, he brandished his frightening stick. They're still looking at you curiously, he thought, as though you weren't born in this quarter, right in Shardaha. But then it seemed that criminals were the only things people remembered. As a young man of twenty, he had worked as a saddler; his hobby was playing marbles under the mulberry tree. He was an orphan, and only had a place to sleep in the saddlery because of the charity of Amm Zahra who owned it. The first time he carried hot oil to Lahluba's house, the latter had cuffed him on the neck. That was the way he greeted him. How beautiful Zainab had been. If it weren't for that tyrant Lahluba, she would have been your wife for the past twenty years. He could have asked for her hand before you did, but he only took a fancy to her on the wedding night. The clubs had been smashed, the singer ran away and the musical instruments were broken. You were set upon like a receptacle or a piece of furniture. You weren't weak or a coward, but it was more than you could do to resist. He had thrown you to the ground at his feet and scores of feet had surrounded you. He had laughed deadly. "So here's the groom," he had said mockingly, "with his hot oil!"

Your new *gallabiyya* had been torn, the skull cap had been lost and all the rest of your life's savings had been stolen.

"I'm from Shardaha, Sir. We're all your men, under your protection."

He cuffed him on the neck which was his normal way of showing affection. "What shall we do with him, scum?!" he asked his men mockingly.

"I'm your servant, Sir," he replied, "but please let me go...."

"Is your bride waiting for you?"

"Yes, Sir. And I want my money. It doesn't matter about the *gallabiyya*...."

He grabbed you by the hair and pulled you forward. "Sharshara!" he said in a new tone of voice, serious and terrifying.

"At your command, Sir."

"Divorce her!"

"What?"

"I told you to divorce her. Divorce your bride, now...."

"But...."

"She's beautiful, but life is even more so!"

"I only married her this afternoon."

"Well, you'll be divorcing her tonight. Such things are best done quickly!"

He had sighed in despair. Lahluba kicked him harshly. In seconds, they stripped him of his torn clothes. He fell to the ground with a blow on his neck. He was beaten with a cane till he lost consciousness and then his face was put into a pit full of horse urine.

"Divorce her!" Lahluba said again. He wept from pain, grief and humiliation, but did not utter a word.

"No one will ask you for alimony in arrears," Lahluba said in a tone of mocking sympathy.

One of Lahluba's henchmen shook him roughly. "Thank God," he said, "and show your gratitude to your master!"

Pain, humiliation, and a lost bride. And now here were the smells of the streets and bazaars of Ala to carry you back into the past even more than the actual return itself did. The old playgrounds and Zinab's face which you had loved ever since she was ten years old. For twenty years, envy had been the only emotion to stir your heart. Up till that time, it had only been love and play. Fairly soon, he thought, I shan't be sighing to have lost the things in life which I lost. When I crush you under my feet, Lahluba, and tell you to divorce her, I'll recover twenty years of my life which have been lost in Hell just like that. I'll also get some consolation for the money I've thrown away on this gang I've brought with me; money I got through hard work, toil, stealing and robbery, and by exposing myself to all kinds of dangers.

When the tunnel which leads to Shardaha loomed up a short distance away, he turned to his men. "Take care of his henchmen," he said, "and leave him to me. Don't harm anyone else."

He did not doubt for a minute that news of this raid of his had already reached Shardaha and that he would soon be standing face to face in front of Lahluba. Now only a short tunnel separated him from his goal. He led them forward cautiously, but they did not come across anyone at ne entrance. Clasping their sticks and letting out terrifying shouts, they plunged forward all at once but found the road in front of them empty. People had taken refuge in houses and taverns. The Shardaha road stretched out ahead of them as far as the wilderness which marked the boundary on the desert side.

"It's a trick," his friend whispered in his ear. "It's a trick, by my Lord, Abu l-Abbas."

"Lahluba doesn't use tricks," Sharshara commented quizzically. "Lahluba," he yelled at the top of his voice, "come out, you coward!"

But nobody answered and no one came out into the road. He looked in front of him in bewilderment, encountering a hot stifling wave of dust as he did so. When would he be relieved of his twenty years of anger and envy?! He saw the short, arched door of the saddlery. It was shut. He moved towards it cautiously and knocked on it with his stick. A quaking voice was heard from inside. "Please let me be!" it yelled pleadingly.

"Amm Zahra," Sharshara yelled triumphantly, "come on. You'll be safe...."

The old man's face appeared in the aperture in the wall above the door. He looked around him feebly.

"Don't be afraid. No one wants to harm you. Don't you remember me?"

The old man looked at him for a long time. "Who are you, may God protect you?" he asked in despair.

"Have you forgotten Sharshara, the young boy who worked for you?"

The blurred eyes widened. "Sharshara?" he yelled. "By God's book it is Sharshara!"

The door was soon opened. The old man hurried towards him and greeted him with open arms although he was secretly frightened. They embraced. Sharshara was patient until the old man had finished. "Where's Lahluba?" he asked.

"Lahluba!"

"Where's the cowardly head of your gang?"

The old man gave a sigh as he raised his head to reveal a thin, emaciated neck. "Don't you know, my son?" he said. "Lahluba died some time ago!"

"No!!" Sharshara cried out from the bottom of his heart as he reeled under this hidden blow.

"It's the truth, my son!"

"No, no, you old windbag!" he said with an even louder and more vicious tone of voice.

"But he is dead," the old man said, stepping back a pace fearfully, "and that's it!"

Sharshara's arms drooped and his body sagged.

"Five years ago or more...." the old man continued.

Alas! Why was it that all creation disappeared leaving only dust behind?

"Believe me," the old man continued, "he's dead. He was invited to a banquet in his sister's house and ate kuskus.*. He and many of his henchmen were poisoned; none of them recovered."

Alas! He found it difficult to breathe. It was as though the atmosphere had changed into bricks. He felt buried in the depths of the earth without knowing how much of him was left above ground. He looked at Amm Zahra with a saddened and dispirited look. "So Lahluba's dead then?"

"Yes. And the rest of his henchmen split up since it was so easy to throw them out...."

"None of them are left?"

"Not one, thank God."

Suddenly he let out a cry like thunder. "Lahluba," he

* boiled cracked wheat

yelled, "you coward, why did you die?!"

The old man cringed at the gruffness in his voice. "Calm down," he begged, "and thank God."

He seemed on the verge of collapse and was about to turn to his companions, but he just stood there listlessly. "What have you heard of Zainab?" he asked.

"Zainab?!" the old man asked in bewilderment.

"Old man, have you forgotten about my bride whom he forced me to divorce on our wedding night?"

"Oh, yes!... She's an egg seller in Donkey Alley!"

Defeated and dejected, he looked at his men, the group on which he had spent his entire life, money and patience. Now here was sheer blindness handing it all over to nothingness. "Wait for me by the mountain," he told them angrily.

His look froze as he faced them. They were disappearing into the tunnel one after another. Would he catch up with them? When would he and why? Would he go back by way of Al-Jawwala or by the wilderness? But Zainab, yes indeed, Zainab. He's used up twenty years of his life for her. Was it really for her?! You won't be getting to her, he thought, over the crushed figure of a tyrant as you imagined. He's dead and there's no point in desecrating graves. How horrible emptiness is! There she is in her shop, she and no one else. Who would have imagined we'd meet in this obscure, feeble and embarrassed fashion!?

He sat down in a tiny cafe the size of a prison cell and started watching the shop which was full of customers. There she was, a strange woman padded with layers of flesh and experience to go with it. The years had matured her simple features. She was wrapped in black from head to toe, but her face had kept a good deal of beauty. There she was haggling and bargaining, exchanging pleasantries and arguing just like an experienced merchant. There she was if you wanted her; you could have her without a struggle, but without honor either. You had lost forever the chance to stand with a foot on Lahluba's chest and order him to divorce her. How horrible emptiness is! He didn't take his eyes off her for a moment. Memories came flooding back and gave him a strange, sad feeling of overwhelming despair. He had no idea of what to do. He believed so much that she was everything in life, and yet where was she?!

Sunset came like the end of life itself. The customers left one by one. Eventually she sat down on a plaited straw chair and started smoking a cigarette. To rid himself of his despair, he decided to throw himself into her hands. He stopped in front of her. "Good evening," he said.

She raised her made-up eyes to look at him, but did not recognize him. "Can I help you?" she muttered carrying on smoking.

"I don't want anything."

She looked at him again, feeling suddenly worried. Their eyes met in a steady gaze. She raised her eyebrows, and the edge of her mouth broke into a sort of smile.

"It's me!"

"Sharshara!"

"The same, but twenty years later! Like a disease."

"Thank God, you're well. Where have you been?"

"In God's country."

"What about a job, family, children?"

"Nothing."

"So you've finally returned to Shardaha."

"It's been a failure."

She looked doubtful and curious.

"Death got here first!" he continued angrily.

"All that's over and gone," she muttered discontentedly.

"Hope was buried with him."

"All that's over and gone."

They looked at each other for a long time.

"How are you?" he asked.

She pointed at the egg baskets. "Just as you can see. Marvellous!!"

There was a moment's pause.

"Didn't...didn't you get married?" he asked.

"My sons and daughters are grown up." A meaningless answer, a weak excuse like a trap.

What would be the point of coming back, he thought, before you've recovered your lost honor? How horrible emptiness is! She pointed to an empty chair in a corner of the shop. "Take a seat," she said.

A sweet sound like bygone days. But only dust was left.

"Another time."

In an agony of despair, he hesitated and then shook her hand and left. This, his only chance in life, had gone and would never be repeated again. That is how it had been for him twenty years ago. But at least that time, hope had not yet been buried. He disliked the idea of going to the mountain by way of Al-Jawwala; he did not want to see anyone or let anyone see him. So there was the road to the wilderness; and that is the one he took, into the wilderness....

Nagib Mahfuz

Mahfuz was born in Cairo in 1911, two years or so before the beginning of the first world war. While he was still a young boy, the family moved from the Al-Husain quarter of Cairo to 'Abbasiyya, a quiet suburb at that time. However, even at this comparative distance from the center of city life and political activity, he was able to watch the uprising against the foreign occupation in 1919. He entered Cairo University during the years of economic depression and graduated with a degree in philosophy in 1934. For a while he worked on the staff of the periodical *Ar-Risala* and translated a book in English on ancient Egypt which was, ironically enough, to be his first published work. During these years, he met Salama Musa, one of the leading figures in the development of socialist ideas in Egypt and a proponent of Darwin's theories in the Arab world. Musa encouraged Mahfuz to write for his journal *Al-Majallat al-Jadida* and helped in the publication of his first collection of short stories, *The Whisper of Madness (Hams al-Junun)* in 1938. Two stories from this collection, the title story and *The Prisoner of War's Uniform*, are included in *God's World*; they show quite convincingly that, while there may be stylistic differences between these and later stories, the ideas which are to be found in many of Mahfuz's recent works were present to some degree from the very outset.

The decade of the 1940's, the war years followed by a period of great political turmoil, was one of considerable writing activity for Mahfuz (the works are discussed below). The revolution of 1952 wrought a great change in Egyptian society, and Mahfuz wrote nothing for several years. Then the publication of his *Trilogy* in 1956 and 1957 brought him fame throughout the Arab world; one of the volumes of this huge work was awarded the State Prize for Literature in Egypt in 1956. The period from 1958 has also been one in which Mahfuz has produced a succession of novels, as well as collections of short stories and plays. His latest novel, *Hubb Tahta l-Matar (Love in the Rain)* has in fact just been published (1973).

While pursuing his writing career, Mahfuz continued to work as a civil servant. In the early 1960's he was director of the Cinema and Theatre Organization, and thereafter was adviser to the Minister of Culture until his retirement in 1971. He is now a regular writer for *Al-Ahram* and continues to publish his short stories and plays in its pages.

The Novels

The first novel of Nagib Mahfuz was published in 1939. entitled 'Abath al-Aqdar (The Fates' Mockery), it was a historical novel set in ancient Egypt, full of action and coincidence. It was followed in 1943 and 1944 by two further examples of this genre, Radubis and Kifah Tiba (The Struggle of Thebes). While Kifah Tiba is probably the most successful of these three early works from the point of view of structure and characterization, it is Radubis which is usually singled out because of the way in which the author seems to be using the character of the king, Menenra, as a means of criticizing the less savoury antics of King Faruq in Egypt during the 1940's.

Some commentators record that Mahfuz intended to produce a whole series of novels set in ancient Egypt. However, in 1945 there appeared the first in a series of works which depict with great accuracy and attention to detail the life in the older quarters of the city of Cairo*. These appeared at the rate of one every year until 1949 when Mahfuz em-barked on his largest work to date, Ath-Thulathiyya (The Trilogy). Al-Qahirat al-Jadida (Modern Cairo) – as this first novel was called – introduced Mahfuz' realistic phase in which he set himself to portray the structure of Egyptian society and the social conditions of its various classes. Mahgub, the hero of this work, is a poor student who grad-uates without being able to find a job. With the help of a "friend", a deal is arranged whereby

* Midaq Alley (Beirut, 1966) is a translation by Trevor Le Gassick of Zugag al-Midagg (1947).

he will marry the mistress of a senior official and be given a post as a civil servant in exchange. He accepts the offer, but, when his opportunistic rise in status arouses his "friend's" resentment, the arrangement is revealed to the senior official's wife and a scandal results. As a general background to this story, we can see the widespread predominance of the old political parties on the fabric of Egyptian society. Among the most successful of these novels is *Bidaya wa Nihaya* (*Beginning and End*) which was published in 1949. At the very outset of the narrative we learn of the death of a civil servant and the consequent hardships for his family. The wife tries to maintain the household as best she can, but circumstances and the activities of her children make this very difficult. Hasan, the eldest son, is heavily involved with thugs and gangsters on the night-club scene. Husain, one of two younger sons, gets himself a position as a school clerk so that he can support himself, his younger brother Hasanain, and their mother and sister. Unknown to him, Nafisa, the sister, is working as a seamstress and occasional prostitute. When Husain finds this fact out, he forces her to commit suicide by jumping into the Nile and then follows her himself.

All these novels portray their characters in quite vivid detail, but equally important in every case is the attention paid to the description of the quarter in which the work is set and the way in which the lives of the characters blend in with their surroundings. Their lives are filled with real tragedies, be it on the scale of the general effect on Egypt of the second world war or on the more personal level of the family disasters in works like *Beginning and End*. Some try to break out of the environment in which they live, others submit to whatever Fate has willed for them and yet carry on their lives with a good deal of resilience.

This series of novels culminates in *The Trilogy* (*Ath-Thulatthiyya*, 1956-7), a work which won for its author the State Prize for Literature in Egypt and the esteem of the entire Arab world. It paints a picture of Egypt during the years 1918 to 1944 through the eyes of a single family, the members of which branch out in many directions in the course of three succesive generations. In the first volume, the patera-familias, 'Abd al-Gawwad, rules his family with an iron hand although he does not restrict his own desires for wine or woman in a similar fashion. In the second volume which is set in a different quarter of Cairo, the figure of Kamal, one of 'Abd al-Gawwad's sons, emerges. He goes to a teachers' college, reads the works of Darwin and suffers a crisis of belief which leads to a fearsome argument with his father. On a political level too, Kamal finds himself losing hope in the effectiveness of the old party system with its falsified concept of democracy. Meanwhile, the sons and daughters of the family have married, and the third generation begins to appear. In the last volume which is set in a third quarter, much attention is devoted to two grandsons whose activities seem to reflect much of the intellectual and political turmoil of the period. Unlike Kamal, their beliefs are positive and assertive. Both of them act; one belongs to the Muslim Brethren, an extremely reactionary religious group, while the other is a Communist and works for a leftist newspaper. At the end of the work, both are in jail because of their views, and Egypt's confusion in the period before the revolution is clearly reflected in the fate of these two young men.

This huge work of fifteen hundred pages succeeds to a remarkable degree in portraying the lives of the members of the family of 'Abd al-Gawwad while incorporating them within the political events and intellectual movements which occurred in Egypt during the timespan of this work. In a sense, Time, the great destroyer, the great healer, is the main hero of this work; the members of 'Abd al-Gawwad's family play their roles in their own lifetimes, political events occur, intellectual turmoil stirs up the young, and yet Time carries on regardless.

The Trilogy was completed, so Mahfuz informs us, in April, 1952. In July of that year, the Egyptian revolution occurred; King Faruq was banished, and soon a new regime came to power. Mahfuz published nothing for a number of years, claiming later that the society which he had been describing had changed drastically and that he did not feel confident enough to portray the new revolutionary society which was emerging. When he did publish a new work in 1959, it was indeed controversial but not for the way in which it reflected the new Egyptian society in particular. *Children of Our Quarter (Awlad Haritna)* appeared in serial form in the daily newspaper *Al-Ahram* (where many of his more recent works have first appeared) and gave in allegorical form a version of mankind's religious history using thinly disguised names for the major figures. The first of the sons of Jabalawi (God), for example, is named Adham, a close approximation to Adam, while one of his descendants is called Jabal, the Arabic word meaning 'mountain' in a clear reference to Sinai and Moses. Such personifications of God and the prophets coupled with the implication that science, in the form of a later descendant 'Arafa, has destroyed God, aroused the intense opposition of the conservative religious establishment in Egypt, and as a result the work was not published in book form there, although it has since appeared in Lebanon.

During the 1960's, Mahfuz published a whole series of novels which reflect the changing nature of Egyptian society in the post-revolutionary period and display an increasing concern with the individual and his role in and response to the society of which he is a part. These novels are characterized by a greater economy of description and also by the use of the stream of consciousness technique with considerable effect. *In The Thief and the Dogs (1961)* for example, we are let into the nightmarish world of Sa'id Mahran who is released from prison at the beginning of the novel and who, in trying to take vengeance on his wife and her lover who contrived to put him there, murders two other people by mistake and is hounded to death by the police. In *Chatter on the Nile (1966)*, we even experience the fantasies, daydreams and nightmares of the same character who spends most evenings on his houseboat with a group of friends in a drugged stupor. It is this character who is told by a figure from ancient Greek lore that "these are times of war and misery". As if to prove his point, the June war of 1967 and its aftermath proceeded to devastate the Arab world both physically and mentally. Mahfuz again stopped writing novels and turned his attention to short stories (some of which appear in this collection) and plays.

Most recently (1972-3), Mahfuz has published two works under the general rubric of *riwaya*, 'story' or 'novel'. The first, entitled *Al-Maraya (Mirrors)*, seems to be more in the nature of a fictional intellectual and political history of Egypt during the author's own lifetime portrayed through a series of fifty-four characters from various walks of life who 'mirror' the society in which they live. *Al-Hubb Tahta l-Matar (Love in the Rain)* reflects much of the current malaise in Egypt, being set in Cairo while some of the male characters are also fighting and being wounded or killed at the Suez Canal front. The comments voiced by some of the characters about the stark contrast between life at the front and the seeming indifference of the majority of the population in the city would seem to be painting an accurate picture of the situation in Egypt today.